"If we'd known we were going to make it, the challenge would not have been the same — we might not have gone. If we'd known what lay ahead, we *certainly* would not have gone.

"We encountered hundreds of species of creatures including snakes, crocodiles, piranhas, sharks, whales, bees, and scorpions. We were arrested, shot at, robbed, jailed, and set upon by pirates. Our skin was baked to scab by the sun and we were close to starvation several times.

"Strangely enough, the only animal that gave us any trouble was man."

* * * * *

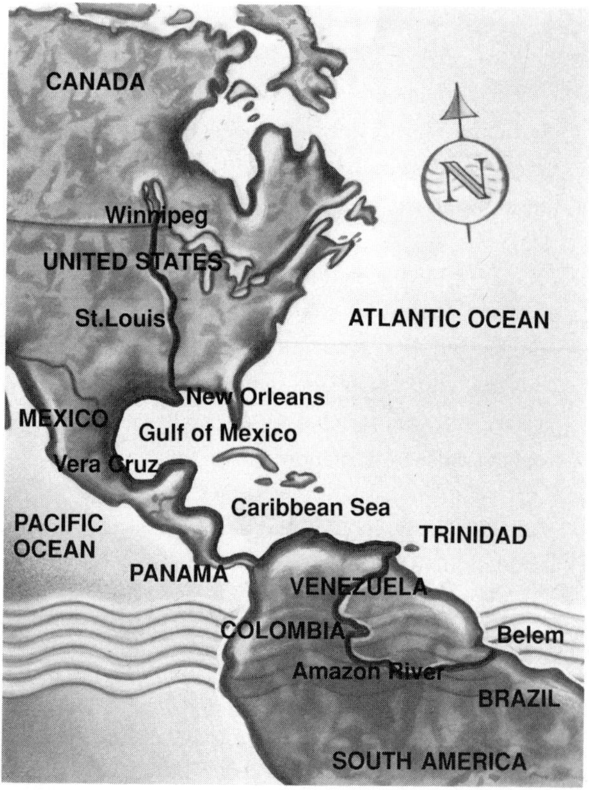
CANADA
Winnipeg
UNITED STATES
St.Louis
ATLANTIC OCEAN
New Orleans
MEXICO
Gulf of Mexico
Vera Cruz
Caribbean Sea
PACIFIC
OCEAN
TRINIDAD
PANAMA
VENEZUELA
COLOMBIA
Belem
Amazon River
BRAZIL
SOUTH AMERICA

NELSON NOVELS

PADDLE TO THE AMAZON

THE AMAZING CANOE ADVENTURE

Don Starkell
Edited by Charles Wilkins

Nelson Canada

Published in 1990 by
Nelson Canada,
A Division of International Thomson Limited
1120 Birchmount Road
Scarborough, Ontario M1K 5G4

Series Editor: Sharon Siamon

Editor: Sandra Manley
Art Director: Lorraine Tuson
Series Design: Gail McGowan
Cover Design: Gail McGowan
Cover Illustration: Sharon Foster
Maps: James Loates Illustrating
Map on page 2: Tracy Walker
Printing: Best Gagné Book Manufacturers

Canadian Cataloguing in Publication Data

Starkell, Don
Paddle to the Amazon

(Nelson novels)
Young adult ed.
ISBN 0-17-603059-X

1. Starkell, Don, 1932- -Juvenile literature.
2. Starkell, Dana - Juvenile literature. 3. Canoes and canoeing - America - Juvenile literature.
4. America - Description and travel - 1981 - - Juvenile literature. I. Wilkins, Charles. II. Title.

E27.5.S73 1990 j910.4 C90-093010-1

Printed and bound in Canada
4567890/GP/543

TABLE OF CONTENTS

1	Leaving Home	9
2	Into the U.S.A.	15
3	Down the Mississippi	25
4	Beaten by the Gulf	31
5	Picking Up the Pieces	41
6	A New Start with Gabby	47
7	Out of Mexico	57
8	At Gunpoint in Honduras	64
9	The Nicaraguan War Zone	75
10	Into Colombia	82
11	The Evil Coast	87
12	Venezuelan Feast and Famine	96
13	To the Dragon's Mouth	103
14	Interlude in Trinidad	108
15	Farewell to the Sea	116
16	Up the Orinoco	124
17	On to Brazil	129
18	Down the Rio Negro	136
19	On the Amazon	142
20	Journey's End	150
	Epilogue	158

This book is dedicated to all those who helped us on our way — and to our detractors, too. Without them our determination would not have been the same.

Editor's Preface to the Original Edition

I first crossed paths with Don Starkell in 1983. He told me that he had a manuscript — a diary — written between 1980 and 1982, while he was canoeing from Winnipeg to South America with his son, Dana. He said, "I wonder if you'd take a look at the thing. I'd like to make a book of it; I need some advice."

A few days later he handed me a huge stack of pages. I flipped through the pile and handed it back. "I can't read it," I apologized. "You'll have to type it out." I was sure I'd never see the manuscript again.

I have since learned not to underestimate a man who can guide a canoe halfway around the world. Three months later, the typing was done — by Don himself; almost four kilograms of paper, 1,400 pages, densely typed. A million words in all.

It is an incredible story — both inspired and inspiring — and I am proud to be connected with it.

CHARLES WILKINS

Preface to this Edition

When we contacted Dana Starkell in the autumn of 1989, he was working on his fourth album of guitar music, to be titled "The Fantastic Voyage." Dana's guitar was lashed to the top of the canoe, all the way from Winnipeg to the mouth of the Amazon River. At times, when the canoe was paralyzed by ocean storms, or stuck fast in the mud of a shallow lagoon, Dana says that "practising the guitar made me feel that at least I was moving forward in another direction."

In a way, the guitar seems almost a symbol of the Starkells' courage and determination. It was stolen, crushed, and washed overboard many times, but each time Dana managed to rescue it and carry on.

It is our hope that many readers of this edition of *Paddle to the Amazon* will be inspired to read the original book and explore in greater detail the amazing story of Don and Dana's historic voyage.

SHARON SIAMON

CHAPTER 1

Leaving Home

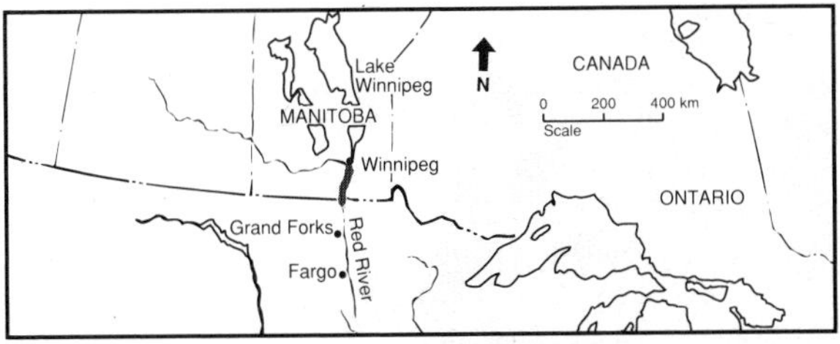

If we'd known we were going to make it, the challenge would not have been the same — we might not have gone. If we'd known what lay ahead, we *certainly* would not have gone.

On reaching Belém, Brazil, nearly two years after our departure, I would write in my diary: "We have taken some 20 million paddle strokes to get here and have travelled every variety of waterway. We have slept on beaches, in jungles, in fields — sometimes in the canoe, on the open water. We have shared simple food and lodgings; we have dined aboard million-dollar yachts. We have encountered hundreds of species of creatures: snakes, crocodiles, piranhas, sharks, whales, bees, and scorpions. Strangely enough, the only animal that has given us any trouble is man; we have been arrested, shot at, robbed, jailed, and set upon by pirates. We have capsized fifteen times at sea and forty-five times our canoe has been broken on rocks or reefs. Our skin has been baked to scab by the sun. We have been close to starvation.

"In spite of all we've endured, our arrival here in Belém was anything but triumphal. No banners, no champagne, no tears or kisses. Nobody at all.... Perhaps we deserve such a fate. We have come too far."

Our departure date was set for June 1, 1980. The night before, we moved our canoe and supplies from our home in north Winnipeg to the bank of the Red River nearby.

Next morning, we exchanged our final kisses and hugs, and climbed into the canoe. About ten metres from shore, I turned and waved, bound for South America. I was proud, I was hopeful, I was scared.

I was also immediately aware that we were somewhat overloaded. We had *everything* in that canoe, including a tent, tarps, two spare paddles, three gas stoves, fuel, tools, first-aid kit, canoe-repair kit, radio, cameras, tape recorder, binoculars, sleeping shells, food, and clothing. We had books on electronics so that Jeff could continue the electronics studies he'd begun in high school. Riding on top of the load, was Dana's classical guitar, well waterproofed in a vinyl case.

Our overall weight was a numbing 470 kg. In the excitement of the moment, however, we forged into the current as if paddling a 25 kg racing shell.

Our first strokes that morning were the culmination of ten years of planning. Following the break-up of my marriage in 1970, I realized we needed a long-range plan of some sort that would carry us purposefully into the future.

A plan emerged — at first a kind of fantasy plan. Somewhere down the line, when the boys were old enough, we would take a monumental canoe trip. I had always been fascinated by the great travels of Columbus and Cortés, of Orellana and von Humboldt, and, in more recent years, of Papillon, on the rivers of South America.

By late 1970, I had made up my mind — or more accurately, had made up my imagination. We would travel south from Winnipeg via the Red River and the Mississippi; along the Intracoastal Waterway of the Gulf of Mexico, and the coast of Central and South America; 1600 kilometres up the Orinoco River; 1300 kilometres down the Rio Negro; and 1600 kilometres down the Amazon. The route would cover nearly 20 000 kilometres and would take us two years to complete. If we made it, it would be the longest canoe trip ever. Could we do it? I had no idea.

During the ten years that followed, hundreds of winter evenings were spent mapping and researching. Summer vacations were spent canoeing and testing equipment. One stint in northern Canada proved that we could easily carry a month's supply of food. Other trips told us that a standard five metre canoe would be far too small.

Finally, we ordered one that was almost six and a half metres in length with an 85 cm beam. It was bright orange in colour and just over 45 kg in weight. We decided to name it after the first white man to navigate the Amazon River in 1541, Francisco de Orellana. So *Orellana* it was.

I built four (almost) watertight aluminum boxes for our food and gear. When in place, they allowed just over two metres of sleeping space at either end of the canoe, while the top of the boxes made a third sleeping spot.

During the late 1970s, I primed my sons constantly for our great adventure, doing everything I could to erase their occasional doubts.

Hundreds of people have asked me, *Why did you go?* To begin to explain, I must briefly jump back to the year 1939, when I was six years old, living with my father, sister, and stepmother in a tiny frame house in the north end of Winnipeg. One of my clearest recollections is the kitchen wood stove, where my sister and I huddled on winter mornings as we cooked up a pot of oatmeal for ourselves before going to school.

In 1939, my father's negligence was brought to the attention of the Children's Aid Society, and a few weeks later a judge offered my sister and me the choice of returning home or going to live in the Children's Home. We chose the Children's Home.

Looking back, I can see that, even by the age of eight or nine, I had developed a need to *be* somebody. My ambitions were to be the fastest runner, the best climber, the strongest swimmer. One day, for no other reason than to test my endurance, I jumped into the Red River in Winnipeg and swam twenty kilometres to Lockport.

Then the Roberts family took me, and a wonderful thing happened: I discovered the canoe. My new family lived on a creek, and, especially in spring when the waters were flooding, I could get into Eric Roberts's canoe and paddle great distances in any direction. I felt free, independent, self-sufficient. When I was paddling that canoe, I was in control.

In the spring of 1950, Winnipeg, a city of nearly half a million people, suffered a disastrous flood, and for a couple of weeks I spent a good deal of time paddling up and down our street, delivering bread and milk to stranded neighbours. Later that summer, I began competing in canoe and kayak races.

Over the next couple of decades, I would compete in hundreds of races but none of these compared to the Centennial trans-Canada canoe race in 1967. In May of that year, ten teams of six paddlers, set out from Rocky Mountain House in Alberta. A hundred and four days later, our Manitoba team reached the Expo 67 site at Montreal, victorious.

Now it was 1980, and we were preparing for a trip which made the 5300 km Centennial race look like a recreational jaunt. Dana was 19, Jeff, 18.

As the days were counted down, I had two main worries. One was the state of Dana's health. For twelve years, Dana had been severely asthmatic. At times I'd seen him blue with wheezing. I believed in my heart, however, that the months of steady exercise would improve his lungs. If the plan backfired, I'd have a lot to answer for.

My other major concern was that Jeff had become a serious student of electronics. Now that he was graduating from high school, he feared the effect of a two-year break in his studies. What's more, he didn't like the idea of abandoning his circle of friends. At no time could I allow myself to think that Jeff would pull out on us. The truth was, we needed him badly. He is a skilled athlete, also an electronics wizard and a talented mechanic. More than anything, of course, we needed him as a son and brother.

Now we were on the Red River, and by mid-afternoon on that first day, our heavy load and our lack of conditioning had begun to tell. We were as crotchety as chickens. By the time we'd gone 40 km upstream, we could barely pull another stroke. Our goal for the day was 50 km to the park at St. Adolphe, so we kept going until, at about 5:30, we dragged ourselves ashore.

By 9:30 p.m. Jeff and Dana were zonked out in the tent. I was literally aching to join them, but not before I'd opened my notebook and recorded my impressions of our first day on the water.

CHAPTER 2

Into the U.S.A.

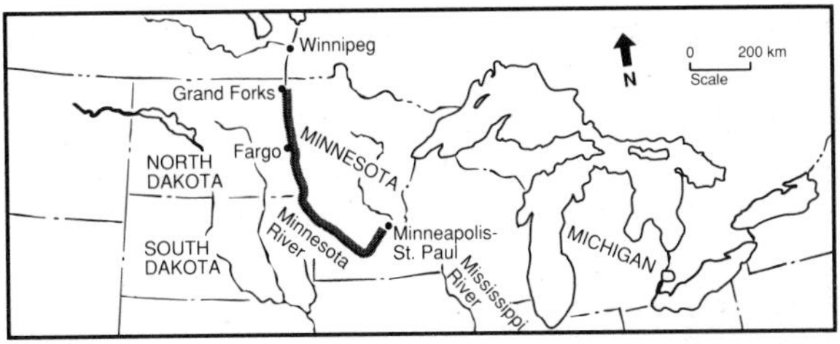

JUNE 5: *on the Red River, south of the American border*

Five days out of Winnipeg, and my concerns have shifted rather drastically from the trip at large to the battles of the moment. Dana is not himself; he is pale, his face thin, his expression blank. His asthma has caught up with him, and for much of the day I could hear his heavy wheezing from the bow seat. Most of the time he just sat, occasionally trying a stroke or two. In the mid-morning Jeff moved into the bow, and Dana took the #2 seat. Even now, Dana is sitting listlessly on the ground, unable to practise his guitar, which has put him in a foul mood. He couldn't help us unload the canoe this afternoon, and has barely been able to eat, as he's constantly sucking for air. He's going to try to get through the night without medication, and has decided to sleep in the open air while Jeff and I occupy the tent.

With the river narrowing and the current increasing against us as we move upstream, our reduced power is all the more costly. On the afternoon of the 3rd, at the Roseau River Indian bridge, the water was so fast and boulder-strewn, it brought us to a halt in a small set of rapids. We were forced to swing the canoe around and retreat through the boulders. We fluked the retreat without damage and took another run at the current. It was futile. In the 30°C heat, our weary arms and backs wouldn't propel us, and we were obliged to portage. We decided to camp for the night. Had we swamped, *Orellana* would have been broken on the rocks; our canoe is of sturdy fibreglass construction, but it's only 1.6 mm thick and no match for rocks.

Already we've encountered a profusion of wildlife: snapping turtles, owls, hawks, white-tail deer, enormous catfish, and suckers spawning in the shallows. A bit of the area's natural history revealed itself today. At various points along the river bank, ancient buffalo bones (mostly skulls and horns) protruded from the clay. Some were buried under one and a half to three metres of soil. Paddling up this Red River, with its heavily treed banks, can't be much different from what it was 200 years ago when the buffalo grazed by the numberless thousands in these parts.

Our plan is to get to Minneapolis, 1300 km to the south, by July 1st. But before Minneapolis, we have nearly 650 km of upstream paddling on the Red. From the source of the Red, we'll travel the Bois de Sioux River, then a series of lakes and reservoirs will take us into the Minnesota River. At Browns Valley, Minnesota, we'll portage the height of land that forms the Continental Divide. The Divide separates two great water systems: the north-flowing waters that lead to Hudson Bay and the Canadian Arctic, and the fabled Mississippi and its tributaries, which flow south to the Gulf of Mexico.

It is now 9:30 p.m., and as Dana and Jeff sleep, I lie waiting for the ten o'clock news on our all-weather Sony radio. Weather reports have never been more important.

JUNE 6: *on the Red River south of Hallock, Minnesota*

During the night, all I could hear was Dana's laboured breathing from the canoe nearby. He got little or no sleep. Today he sat amidships, while Jeff and I worked like galley slaves. Jeff didn't complain, putting his full heart into the additional challenge. But I know now that we can't go on this way. We're wearing down badly, and have come only 270 km. I'm so drained, emotionally and physically, I'm afraid I won't be able to sleep.

Our goal for the day was Drayton, North Dakota, and in mid-afternoon, after hours of paddling, we passed a couple of bearded yokels on shore who told us the Drayton dam was only a couple of kilometres ahead. Our hearts lifted — we could look forward to an early day. A few kilometres gradually turned into 15, and our optimism turned into despair, as we snaked around bend after bend into the stiff current. At seven o'clock, after eleven hours on the water, we landed and pitched our tent outside town. Our long day's labour had gained us 48 km.

JUNE 9: *on the Red River south of Big Woods, Minnesota*

What a difference a few days make. Dana has more or less returned to health and is again taking his share of the paddling. The river is no kinder to us, however, and our days are as exhausting as ever.

We are now two days behind schedule and are dismayed by our slow progress. Even the pleasures of stopping to camp have been spoiled by the slimy clay of the river banks. To make things worse, we are sunburnt — particularly our faces. Our lips are parched, and we've all been peeling large chunks of cremated skin from our noses. We haven't bathed properly in nine days.

Nevertheless, our spirits are high. The weather was near-perfect today, and as I sit on one of our equipment boxes writing, a warm sun is peeking over the treetops from the other side of the river in North Dakota. Against the challenge of the current, we are rounding into shape. Jeff and Dana are showing new muscles daily, and we're paddling at a better clip.

Our spirits are such tonight that we really believe we can do what we set out to do.

JUNE 11: *on the Red River south of Grand Forks, North Dakota*
Reached Grand Forks yesterday morning, and Jeff and Dana raced to the YMCA for showers. This morning I awoke to the music of Bach, as Dana practised his guitar outside the tent. As we were about to pull out around nine o'clock, we were surrounded by media — television, newspaper, radio — all wanting interviews. By 10:30 we finally got away, trailed to the river bank by a string of reporters.

We were bothered throughout the day by numerous biting insects. The heat and sun dehydrate us, and we've each been consuming four litres or so of water a day.

JUNE 17: *Fargo, North Dakota*
Our hard days of paddling in the heat have begun to catch up to us — mentally as well as physically. During the first hour of paddling yesterday morning I could feel our speed lagging. The current was strong, the water shallow. In many places, fallen trees and debris blocked the flow. We began to see the bloated bodies of cows and pigs and dogs among the filth along shore. The smell was atrocious. Everything started getting to me. I paddled harder and called for more steam up front. When I didn't get it I blew up and threw my paddle into the canoe. "Why should I kill myself while you guys loaf?" I shouted.

"Why should we kill ourselves?" said Jeff.

The boys shut down, and we sat in the shallows for half an hour doing nothing.

I gradually cooled out and apologized, and

for the rest of the day Jeff and Dana paddled like giants — all the way to Fargo, where we pitched camp at about ten o'clock. We had paddled nearly fifteen hours and had advanced only 43 km. We sat at a picnic table in the dark and stuffed ourselves with macaroni, canned peaches, and fruit cocktail. Later, as I lay in the tent, I could think only of the Mississippi, whose southbound current will give us a free ride all the way to New Orleans.

I continue to lose weight and am having trouble gaining muscle tone. Too much daily work and my age won't allow me to develop as in years gone by. I sit behind the boys and watch their shoulders and backs develop almost by the hour.

JUNE 22: *on the Bois de Sioux River*
Three weeks out of Winnipeg, and this morning at eight o'clock we came to the end of our battle with the Red River. The past few days have been anything but easy. The current has been fierce, the insects have been vicious, and Dana has been sick again.

As we reached the headwaters of the Red, the Ottertail River appeared from the east, the pretty Bois de Sioux from the south. I got out on a bridge at the junction and sent Jeff and Dana up the Ottertail, so that I could film them coming back into the Red. It was a sweet moment for us, 800 km into our trip. By the time we camped this afternoon, we had covered 56 km, one of our best days yet. An hour ago, Jeff and I gave in to the 30°C heat and took a dip, while Dana practised guitar in the steamy tent.

JUNE 26: *on the Minnesota River, south of Ortonville, Minnesota*

Our route over the past few days has taken us across the Continental Divide. For our portage over the height of land, we packed the canoe and equipment on a trailer borrowed from a hospitable tourist resort, and Jeff and I harnessed ourselves in like horses. We could have saved ourselves a lot of time by putting the canoe on the back of a pick-up truck. But we promised ourselves months ago that our entire journey would be achieved under our own power. No lifts, no tows.

The portage was tough. Our load was poorly balanced, and for eight kilometres we sweated and strained, our padded rope harness cutting into our shoulders. Dana wheezed along behind, but by the time we reached the Little Minnesota River, he was breathing easier, having apparently benefited from the walk.

We began strongly this morning, with 32 breezy kilometres on Big Stone Lake. But within minutes of finding our way through the reeds onto the Minnesota River at Ortonville, we were in the worst mess of our trip. The water was shallow, dirty, and heavily blocked with deadfall trees and boulders. Finally, Jeff and I walked to a nearby farm belonging to a couple named Gayle and Colleen Hedge.

We noticed an old farm wagon in the yard.

"Would you mind if we used it?" I asked.

"Be my guest," said Gayle, "but it weighs almost 600 kg, and I don't think you're gonna get far with it."

We placed our canoe upside down on the wagon. We then loaded in our equipment and hitched steering reins to the pull bar. Dana climbed onto the canoe and took the reins. Jeff and I got behind the wagon and began to push. Our load, which now weighed over 900 kg, groaned across the yard.

Cars and trucks passed us from ahead, blasting their horns in disbelief at seeing Dana coming down the highway on top of this monstrous wagon, driving a team of non-existent horses (Jeff and I were out of sight behind the wagon).

In all we pushed almost ten kilometres. The wagon nearly got away from us on the downhill grade to the river, and only by digging our heels hard into the gravel were we able to prevent it from crashing. Dana sat high on his perch, apparently in shock.

Tonight we are happy beyond belief, almost giddy with pride over our big achievement. We cannot be stopped and are now on our downhill route to Minneapolis and the Mississippi.

JUNE 27: *on the Minnesota River*
Although our route today was shown as a "canoe route" on the map, I have *never* encountered worse paddling conditions — stagnant water, endless barricades of deadfall trees, swarms of hungry mosquitoes. At times I had to get out of the canoe into waist- or chest-deep water and hack through the branches and trunks with my axe. Tiny black leeches feasted on my legs, making open, painless wounds that bled freely. At

one point the deadfall made a two-metre wall, and we had to unpack and portage over the top.

At 9:30 p.m., having come a measly 27 km in 15 hours, we pitched camp and crawled into the tent. I lay silently cursing the Minnesota Department of Natural Resources for showing the distance we'd paddled as a canoe route. Had their mapmakers never been here? At the same time, I felt that no conditions could possibly be worse and that, having persevered, we were probably the tougher for it.

JUNE 30: *on the Minnesota River*

By late this afternoon, we had knocked off a fantastic 70 km, for our best day yet. We had also had our biggest thrill, as we shot Patterson's Rapids during the mid-morning. As we approached the rapids, we cut through some large standing waves and roared downhill. *Orellana* shot through the water like an orange missile, and Jeff let out an excited whoop. As our ride ended, Jeff turned to me with a big grin and said, "Let's go again."

"We're not going again!" blurted Dana.

The reactions were so typical of the boys' personalities. Jeff loves sport and speed. As a kid, he used to ride his bike as if he were a circus performer. Dana's main interests have always been art and nature. As a youngster, Dana kept pets, and often spoke of going to the jungle where he could live with the animals. "How are you going to get there?" I'd ask him, and he'd say confidently, "I'm going to walk." Now here he is on his way to the jungle — we'll hope there's not too much walking involved.

We have been on the water a month and have covered 1200 km.

JULY 6: *Minneapolis, Minnesota*
Conditions have improved steadily, and early this afternoon, we reached the first major milestone of our trip — the twin cities of Minneapolis and St. Paul. Our first taste of the cities came yesterday morning, when a helicopter from WCCO TV in Minneapolis came bearing down on us. They had heard about our trip and wanted to interview us. After a half-hour session in front of the television camera, we paddled off with the helicopter chasing us downstream, the cameraman strapped to the outside. They dropped to within six metres of us, and the canoe shook as the big propeller blades lifted the water into peaks.

We were up and away early this morning, anxious to see the Mississippi. In the early afternoon, we passed what appeared to be a large island on our left. We knew we were close to Minneapolis, as powerboats were everywhere. A speedboat skidded by, and the driver hollered, "We saw you guys on television last night!" We asked how far we were from the Mississippi and were surprised to find we'd been on it for five kilometres. The island we'd passed a while back had been the forks. We had reached the Mississippi without knowing it!

CHAPTER 3

Down the Mississippi

JULY 10: *Winona, Minnesota, on the Mississippi River*

Three days out on the Mississippi. The river is travelled by hundreds of pleasure craft and industrial barges.

While our progress has been good (184 km in three days), it's not as rapid as we had hoped. The river is regularly slowed by lift locks and dams. Already we've come through six locks, which dropped from two to four metres each.

The heat wave continues, with today's temperatures again around 35°C.

JULY 26: *at Alton, Illinois, on the Mississippi River*
During our long days on the Mississippi we've settled into a number of routines. We rise well before sunrise, and, while Jeff strikes the tent and packs the equipment boxes, I boil up water on our little army stove, and Dana and I prepare a simple breakfast. When we're ready to go, Dana is first into the canoe, followed by Jeff, leaving me to shove off. Dana sets the stroke — anywhere up to 40 long, deep working strokes a minute. He and Jeff paddle in unison. I switch sides frequently, as a means of steering the canoe.

Late in the morning, the boys, especially Jeff, start clamouring for lunch. Dana and I keep paddling while Jeff turns at his centre position and pries open our two food boxes. He rapidly prepares whatever we're having, and we eat it as we drift. What's the menu? Today, each of us downed two peanut-butter and jam sandwiches, a banana, a few Fig Newtons, and a Snickers bar. And cup after cup of water. The cooling effect of the river on the bottom of the canoe, and the protection afforded by our white vinyl tarp, have kept our food surprisingly cool. Even our margarine usually stays solid, if a bit soft.

On landing, we unload together, and I generally make supper, while Jeff puts up the tent, and Dana goes off to practise his guitar. Having eaten, Jeff turns to his electronics books, or to the radio, or both. Dana does the dishes and packs up.

Every evening when the sun is almost down I boil up a big pot of tea. I pour Dana and Jeff a mugful each, then pour myself a big peach tin of the stuff. I add three large spoons of sugar and two spoons of powdered milk. I then wrap a thick cloth around the hot tin and carry it into the Mississippi till I'm up to my neck in water. The sand bottom is gentle, and as I stand immersed, I slowly drink the precious fluid.

JULY 31: *Hickman, Kentucky, on the Mississippi River*

The Mississippi has been good to us, and we feel none of the resentment toward it that we felt toward the Red. We do have our little hardships: warm drinking water, Mississippi sand in everything, and of course the heat.

We are wiry and strong and can paddle hour after hour without much strain. Our only bug problems of late have come from horseflies, which follow us as we paddle and like to take chunks out of our hides when they get the chance.

Even in the heat, our progress has been tremendous, and has us bubbling with success. We've been on the water two full months and have logged over 2800 km. This evening it occurred to me that we've come this far without using even a single Band-Aid or aspirin. Lots of sleep, good food, and good water are doing the trick for us.

AUGUST 5: *Memphis, Tennessee, on the Mississippi River*

Even if I never looked at our maps, I'd have no trouble calculating when we're approaching a city. The evening before we arrive, Dana and Jeff invariably have good baths and shampoo their hair, as they did last night, getting ready to impress the girls. Jeff pays more attention to the radio. Dana has less interest; he has his guitar.

Early this afternoon we paddled into Memphis. We landed at the Memphis Yacht Club, and got the manager's permission to pitch our tent.

As we ate supper, Dana heard on the radio that the rock group Queen is in Memphis. He has decided to attend the concert they're to give tonight. Off he went a while ago. Jeff is a bit under the weather and has chosen to stay in camp.

For my part, I sit contemplating the Mississippi. It is far more beautiful and powerful than I'd imagined: I love the wide sweep of the water; the beaches and sand bars and dunes; the landscapes and summer flowers.

It is now after midnight, and Dana has returned, thrilled by the concert. He succeeded in finding the promoter, explained his situation, his love of the guitar and, presto, he was given a stage pass. He also managed a half-hour conversation with the group's lead guitarist, Brian May.

AUGUST 8: *south of Helena, Arkansas, on the Mississippi*

Here we are on a torrid sand bar, half desperate for a breath of cold air. Today's temperature was a new high — 38°C.

Jeff hasn't had a good day. The sun is baking the top of his head, giving him headaches, perhaps even a touch of heatstroke. A while ago, he took a white sailor's hat out of our clothes box, cut out the crown, and sewed it into his peaked visor, which has been giving him very little protection. He then tore apart one of my white shirts for a piece of material to sew onto the back of his hat. He's now parading around in it, with a twinkle in his eye.

Because of the heat, we haven't been closing the tent door, and tonight as we're ready to sleep we're being savaged by hundreds of mosquitoes. We've been saving our mosquito netting "bug house" for the swamps and jungles, but will have to pull it out tomorrow. South America can't be any worse than this.

AUGUST 16: *on the Mississippi River*
When I got up this morning before six, I placed the canoe parallel to the river's edge, partly in, partly out of the water, where it could conveniently be loaded. I began making hot chocolate as Jeff took down the bug house, and Dana went off down the beach trying to walk off an asthma attack.

Suddenly Dana came staggering toward us gasping, "The canoe! The canoe!"

It was about 50 metres offshore, drifting rapidly. I dived into the water in a panic swim, aware of what would happen if the canoe reached the main current.

I had some embarrassing explaining to do when I got back. The old canoeman had gotten careless, and his sons weren't about to let him off the hook. In all, not a banner day. Dana was unable to give us much help because of his asthma.

AUGUST 20: *New Orleans, Louisiana, on the Mississippi River*
Red-Letter Day. In the early afternoon, after 50 km of exhausting work, we paddled into New Orleans, the world's third largest port. At three o'clock we climbed the river bank through bottles, cans, wrecked cars, old mattresses, and dead rats, to the city's famous Audubon Park. The park honours one of the world's great naturalists and nature painters, and we were perplexed that its river boundary was in such bad shape. We picked an open area not far from the park zoo and established camp.

For nearly a month, from August 23 to September 20, the Starkells followed the Intracoastal Waterway from New Orleans to Brownsville, Texas. This series of canals and natural lagoons protected them from the strong winds and pounding surf of the Gulf of Mexico. As the Mexican border got closer, however, they became more and more worried about how the Orellana *would survive the wild waters of the Gulf. They were soon to find out!*

To prepare the canoe for its ordeal on the ocean, the Starkells had a special cover made for the top. It had three cockpits for the paddlers, each with a drawstring at the waist. Chrome-plated clips held the cover to the gunwales.

CHAPTER 4

Beaten by the Gulf

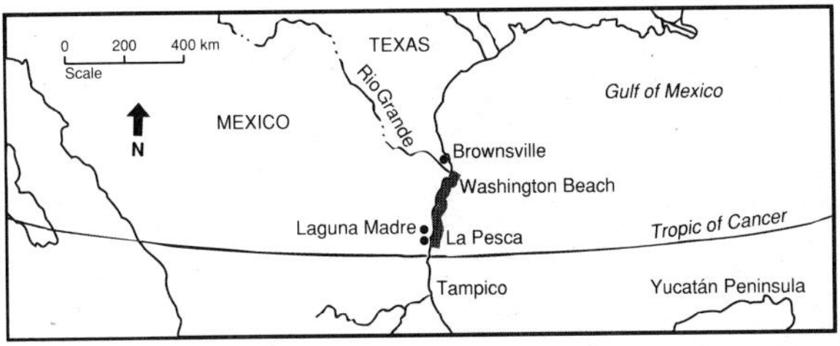

SEPTEMBER 20-22: *Washington Beach, Mexico*
D-day at last, and after breakfast, we walked the canoe nervously to the Gulf of Mexico waterfront. Our load is at absolute maximum, with over 80 litres of drinking water, enough to last us for seven to ten days. We expect no water taps between here and Tampico, Mexico, several hundred kilometres down the coast.

We shoved off at about nine o'clock, paddling slowly and silently. Soon we were on the open sea heading for Mexico.

We paddled for three hours, but by this time

the wind was up, and the swells were getting trickier. "We've gotta go in!" Dana called. "We're not going to make it out here!"

We struggled for another few kilometres, until I knew we had to get off the sea, or we would capsize. "We're going in!" I shouted, swinging toward land. The waves picked us up from behind and drove us hard aground in the shoreline surf nine or ten metres from shore. "Get out and save the canoe and equipment!" I yelled.

Within seconds, we had dragged the swamped canoe ashore, stripped off the cover, and dragged our equipment above the water line. A shallow, tide-fed lagoon runs parallel to the Gulf about 15 metres from the water's edge. It was on the sand between the surf and this lagoon that we decided to make camp.

SEPTEMBER 21: *Washington Beach, Mexico*
One look at the water at dawn told me there would be no paddling today. If anything, the breakers are getting higher.

Late in the morning, desperate to be moving, we tied guide ropes to the copper support brackets in the bow and stern of the canoe and pushed it out into the surf, hoping to drag it through the shallows for a few kilometres. But the breakers smashed into it broadside, and in no time it was half full of water. An hour's tough effort gained us all of a half-kilometre.

We'd barely quit when a military truck appeared behind us. An officer jumped out and ordered five rifle-toting soldiers out of the back. They fanned out and began marching toward us, rifles at the ready. Half an hour of intense interrogation convinced them we were indeed innocent Canadians, and they decided to leave us alone. But not without impressing upon us the absolute importance of dealing shrewdly and convincingly with Latin American police and military personnel. We expect to see plenty more of them.

SEPTEMBER 22: *Washington Beach, Mexico*
Excitement first thing in the morning: the night's high tide had filled our lagoon, and deepened it. It now seemed to extend indefinitely to the south. Too excited to eat, we packed the canoe and began towing it southward. We laughed and celebrated our progress, daring to imagine we could go up to 30 km a day. In no time, however, we were slogging along through muddy water less than two centimetres deep. Disappointed and tired, we again made camp.

As we sit here tonight, we are disguising our feelings well. But I am severely disheartened — the Gulf may have us licked. However, if we can get to Laguna Madre, 80 km south of here, we will have 160 km of protected travel.

SEPTEMBER 23: *Washington Beach, Mexico*
This morning the wind was down, and we saw a chance to get on the sea. We made reasonable progress throughout the morning, but by two o'clock, the seas had begun to build. With the seas mounting, and our control over the canoe slipping, we headed for shore.

About 100 metres out a giant breaker pitched

us forward at a frightful speed. Suddenly we were upside down in the water, thrashing to free ourselves from the drawstrings of our canoe cover. I was the last to surface, powerfully relieved to see two heads bobbing near the overturned canoe. Fortunately, the cover had stayed in place, and we could tow the canoe in as a unit. The only item that escaped was Dana's guitar, which he quickly retrieved.

Ashore, we tore open our equipment boxes, and were dismayed to find everything awash in seawater: passports, maps, radio, clothes, food. We spend hours wiping and wringing and setting things out to dry.

SEPTEMBER 29: *Washington Beach, Mexico*
Nearly a week has passed since I wrote last, and Laguna Madre is as far away as ever. Day after day we sit here, sheltering from the wind and sun, hoping desperately for a sea change. The incredible thing about our enforced stay here is that, in spite of our anxiety and discomfort — in spite of our *thirst* — we haven't panicked or retreated.

Early this afternoon, Dana and I set out to the north, carrying two 20-litre cans and a couple of smaller containers. Eight kilometres of walking in the 30°C heat brought us to a tiny house hidden among the sand dunes. *"Hola!"* we yelled, "Hello!" A tiny Indian woman appeared in the doorway. We explained that we needed water, and her teen-age son, Raul, grabbed our containers and left the house.

Raul returned with our water and proudly

refused our offer of 50 pesos for his effort. After grateful goodbyes, we set off down the beach, staggering along until our arms and shoulders could stand the strain no longer. To make matters worse, we were walking in our bare feet, so that every pebble stung under our increased weight.

A brutal two hours later, we spotted our tent, a welcome blue speck in the distance to the south. Jeff had been watching for us, and it wasn't long before we could see him, a tiny stick-figure, sprinting down the sand towards us. What a pretty sight he was!

The whole complexion of things has changed as we lie here this evening contemplating the sea and sky. Our thirst is quenched, and we can turn our attention to advancing down the coast. For the first time in days, our confidence is high.

SEPTEMBER 30: *Washington Beach, Mexico*
Unfortunately, confidence cannot do for us what a few windless days might. The seas were slightly reduced this morning, so we packed the canoe and launched into the surf. After several kilometres of labour, we found the wind rising, and a rainstorm mounting in the east. We headed for shore. But a powerful side current caught us and in a sickening re-enactment of our previous attempts at sea landings, we were over and treading water in the foaming surf.

Again, everything we owned was soaked: radio, binoculars, flashlight, clothes, maps, documents. *We simply cannot go on this way.*

Late this evening the sea began to mellow, and soon after dark, itching to get a little closer to

Laguna Madre, we put the canoe in the shallow water, and began walking it along the coast. It wasn't easy, as we were continually hit broadside by waves that smashed the canoe against our legs and hips. We stopped every ten minutes to bail.

Sometime close to midnight, we staggered ashore and collapsed. We had gained another three kilometres, and have now come less than ten kilometres in seven days.

OCTOBER 1: *at Mezquital, Mexico*

For the first time in ten days, I can happily report that we are not on Washington Beach. When we wakened this morning, the wind had shifted to the north, giving us a tailwind down the coast.

By mid-afternoon, after seven hours of ocean paddling, we were straining our eyes for any sign of an entrance to the lagoon. Then at about four o'clock we saw a double jetty in the distance, and my heart began thumping with hope. Could this be it?

We were going in anyway. True to form, we were caught by a large wave. For all of 30 seconds, it drove us forward, totally at its mercy, then suddenly plunked us aground, safe on bottom 30 metres from land. We waded ashore and were told by the local fishermen that we were at Mezquital, a new northern entrance to Laguna Madre. I could have screamed for joy. We had made it. We were back in the game.

OCTOBER 3: *on Laguna Madre, Mexico*

This is our second full day on the lagoon. Several times yesterday and today, the water got so shallow we had to get out of the canoe and pull it to deeper water. Nonetheless we've come 80 km, and are now about 80 km out of La Pesca at the south end of the lagoon.

OCTOBER 5: *on Laguna Madre, Mexico*
Just after lunch we met an old fisherman, and tried hard to get information from him about the way and distance to La Pesca. He pointed south, looked me squarely in the eye, and said emphatically, *"No camino! No camino! No camino!"* My translation for *camino* was "road," and we already knew there were no roads to La Pesca from anywhere around here. As we pulled away southward, he shrugged and looked at us with sad frustration.

Within half an hour, the water depth began to decrease dramatically. We were soon grounded in seven centimetres of muddy brine. Our only alternative to sitting there was to get out our ropes and start hauling.

An hour of slugging through the shallows in our bare feet gained us another couple of kilometres. Looking out behind, we could see an endless, snaking trail of little mounds of clay, each one sucked above the water surface by our footsteps.

The hauling grew even more difficult. A frantic hour of sweating and slogging netted us another kilometre, but we could go no further. The only solution was for all of us to stay out here in the mud. With the sun sinking, we climbed back in the canoe and sat silently staring toward La Pesca, about 19 km away.

OCTOBER 6: *on Laguna Madre, Mexico*
Yesterday, while we were hauling, Dana's feet were badly cut by bits of shell and debris. After breakfast, Jeff and I took to the ropes again. Dana called out encouragement and poled with his paddle. Ten steps and rest — twelve steps and rest — nine steps and rest. After a kilometre of this bull labour we gave up. In the heat of the sun we were using up far too much energy and body fluid for what we were achieving.

I held an emergency council. After sunset, Jeff and I would walk south along the Gulf to find water. We were now down to eight litres. We would probably have to go all the way to La Pesca. If things went well, we'd be back tomorrow by sundown. Dana would stay with the canoe.

And so at 7:30, in near-total darkness, we set out, leaving Dana with more than four litres of water and our remaining food. If he kept himself covered and didn't move around too much, the rations would last him two days. It made me sick to leave him there on his own, but he didn't seem to mind.

OCTOBER 7: *on Laguna Madre, Mexico*
By 7:00 a.m. we were standing at the south end of Laguna Madre. La Pesca was a tawdry little place with one paved street and a wandering zoo of cattle, goats, burros, pigs, and chickens.

A few inquiries led us to a man named Israel, who had a jeep and would drive us back to the canoe. Israel told us something that buoyed our hopes: two days of north wind would fill the south end of the lagoon with water of navigable depth. What hope there was of a north wind, a *"norte"* he called it, we had no idea.

The jeep ride back to the canoe cost us 150 pesos, and before Israel left us I had a difficult decision to make. I told him in Spanish that if we weren't in La Pesca in four days, he was to come and get us.

Although I hated to admit it, and hate to admit it now as I write, our odyssey may be over. We can apparently go no further on either the lagoon or the Gulf. Unless the wind changes, in four days we'll have to quit.

Late this evening, I told Dana about the possibility of going to La Pesca by jeep. He stared at me, saying nothing. Jeff spoke up. "I think it's the only thing to do."

"So do I," I said.

OCTOBER 9: *on Laguna Madre, Mexico*

Forty-eight hours have passed since I wrote last, and we have pretty well given up hope for a north wind. We sit here in the mud stew, longing for even a few centimetres of water.

If there's anything even remotely positive about being here, it's that we've had more than enough time for study — Dana his music, Jeff his electronics, and Spanish for me. I sit here in the awful heat, optimistically trying to perfect my Spanish pronunciation.

OCTOBER 10: *Laguna Madre, Mexico*

We have been forced to accept our fate. This morning we made the three-kilometre haul from the centre of the lagoon to the shore of the Gulf.

Dragging the canoe has never been harder, what with the drying mud flats and the condition of our feet. It took us several minutes just to dislodge the canoe from the suction that had built up beneath it. After that, we were dogs, we were mules, we were slaves. Ten steps maximum and rest. And every step sent a jolt of pain up from the bottoms of my feet into my ankles.

After two and a half hours of it, we could go no further. So, with a kilometre to go, we lifted our heaviest equipment box and carried it the rest of the way on its own. Then back for more. The entire operation took four hours.

Our concern now is whether Israel will show up to rescue us at noon tomorrow. If he doesn't appear, Jeff and Dana, whose feet are considerably healthier than mine, will have to walk to town for help.

In spite of the tears I want to shed, I am proud of our accomplishment. No one has ever paddled from Canada to Mexico, and I doubt that anyone will do it again. Jeff and Dana have given their very best to my folly. They are fine sons.

OCTOBER 12: *in La Pesca, Mexico*
Israel came, and we loaded the canoe, and were driven into town.

CHAPTER
5

Picking Up the Pieces

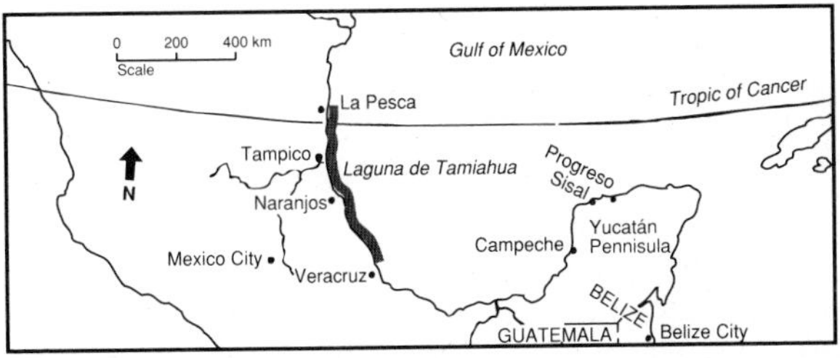

OCTOBER 20: *Veracruz, Mexico*

We left La Pesca in the early morning of the 13th. Israel's neighbour had agreed to drive us the 800 km down the coast to Veracruz where we'll spend the winter. We reached the city at 1:00 a.m. and checked ourselves and our canoe into the ant-infested Roca Mar Hotel.

We spent most of our first week in Veracruz looking for a better place to live. Yesterday a young university student, Gabriel Delgado, sought us out at the Roca Mar, wanting help with his English. As it turned out, he lives in a large private home, where rooms are rented out to students. There was a vacancy, and within an hour we were on our way to see if we could fill it. As we rode the bus, Gabriel, or "Gabby" as he calls himself, told us he studies marine engineering at the university here.

The house was ideal, right on the sea. We soon had our winter home, a second-floor room with use of cooking facilities, and a balcony overlooking the Gulf. What a difference it makes to be among friends and in comfortable, relaxed surroundings.

Meanwhile, I've started to think that maybe our voyage isn't over, maybe we can return to La Pesca under better conditions and pick up where we left off. If nothing develops, we'll return to Winnipeg in the spring.

If I have one apprehension, it's that Jeff has begun to talk about going home. Every so often, he'll drop a comment about missing his friends, or feeling he's not accomplishing anything. Unlike me, he sees no possibility that the trip can continue and has hinted that he'd like to be home by Christmas.

Dana, on the other hand, is looking forward to the weeks of uninterrupted practice time. The Mexican climate is perfect for his asthma; it's been two months since he had any trouble.

NOVEMBER 2: *Veracruz, Mexico*

I'm sad to report that Jeff's departure has become inevitable. This evening as we sat on our beds, he told me frankly that he felt he was wasting his time here. He sees no way that we can go back on the Gulf without disaster. "It's just too crazy out there. It's suicide!" he said.

As hard as it was for me to admit it, I knew in my heart that he was right — it *is* crazy out there; it may well *be* suicidal; it's certainly no place for a canoe.

"If there was any way I thought we could make it, any way at all," he told me, "I'd stay and help." No matter how hard I tried, I couldn't dissuade him.

NOVEMBER 6: *Veracruz, Mexico*

This morning, with tears in our eyes, we said goodbye to Jeff, and he slipped quietly away in a taxi. From Veracruz airport he will fly to Mexico City, then on to Toronto and Winnipeg.

After supper, Dana and I went out for a little walk. We began talking about our predicament, and it occurred to me that if we were going to snap out of our funk we would have to give ourselves a new goal. I said suddenly, "We're going to keep going, Dana. We're going to get a new paddler and keep going."

He looked at me curiously and said, "What if we can't get another paddler?"

"Could I convince you we could do it on our own?"

He gave me one of his patented smiles and said, "I'm willing to try if you are."

NOVEMBER 11: *Veracruz, Mexico*

Our challenge of the past week has been to find someone to take Jeff's place — not an easy task. We phoned an advertisement to our home newspaper, and wrote to several canoeing friends, asking if they'd be interested.

During the past couple of days, however, Gabby himself has become interested in our travels. If he can overcome his fears he just might join us — at least for a while. But those fears are reasonable. He's from an inland town, knows little of the sea, and has never been in a canoe.

NOVEMBER 16: *Veracruz, Mexico*
A few days ago Gabby left to consult his parents about coming with us. We've asked him to join us for the tough portion of the trip from the hated lagoon at La Pesca back along the coast to where we are now.

Sometimes I look at the Gulf and have to work pretty hard to convince myself that it'll be any better in the late winter and spring than it is now. In the meantime, we have three months to spend in Veracruz. So far, I've been enjoying my swimming and snorkelling, and Dana continues to refine his guitar skills. One night, he entertained at a local cantina, playing five or six classical pieces.

NOVEMBER 18: *Veracruz, Mexico*
Gabby returned this afternoon, at least partly committed to the trip. His parents have given their okay, but he still has doubts about his abilities. I spent an hour or so with him this evening, trying to convince him that everything will be fine, that he will have to have faith in himself, and in Dana and me. I think we have our paddler.

DECEMBER 25: *Veracruz, Mexico*
Christmas night, and our lonely thoughts are far away on the snowy Canadian prairie. It is the first time either of us has spent Christmas away from home. We have a pile of Christmas cards from friends back home and those we've met along the route. They all assure us that their thoughts and prayers are with us.

A heavy north wind blew in this morning, stirring the Gulf into mountainous grey swells. Dana and I spent the better part of our day huddling in our room, he with his guitar, I immersed in my Spanish dictionary.

Gabby is now a confirmed member of our crew.

JANUARY 19, 1981: *Veracruz, Mexico*
Our preparations for the trip are progressing. We've moved our departure date forward and will now leave here on February 14, hoping to be in La Pesca the following day. With any luck we should be able to paddle back to Veracruz by March 5 — a stretch of 18 days. That'll give us a big jump on the Gulf, and we'll hope to be out of Mexico by mid-May.

FEBRUARY 7: *Veracruz, Mexico*
A week to go, and I'm beginning to get butterflies. It's like waiting for a race, except this time the feeling is not from excitement but from fear. Both Dana and I have been having nightmares about the sea.

This morning we bought some new tarp clips, some batteries for our radio, and a few

Mexican decals for the canoe. But so far we haven't been able to find other important items — for instance, a bailing pump, and liquid fibreglass for canoe repairs. We applied the new tarp clips and repaired our canoe cover. I managed to get its corroded zippers working again but don't expect they'll last long out on the Gulf.

FEBRUARY 13: *Veracruz, Mexico*

We've done our final grocery shopping and are well stocked with eggs, cheese, ham, margarine, bread, onions, potatoes, chocolate, bananas.

The north wind has been blowing again, and the Gulf is in turmoil, which hasn't done anything for our confidence — but *"el norte"* has presumably made the lagoon navigable again.

Before dawn on the morning of the 14th, Don, Dana, and Gabby, with their canoe and 300 kg of equipment and food, made their way, partly by hitchhiking, to La Pesca. There they met up with Israel, the man who, the previous October, had brought them from Laguna Madre to La Pesca.

CHAPTER 6

A New Start with Gabby

FEBRUARY 16: *La Pesca, Mexico*
By ten this morning we were loaded on our old friend Israel's jeep and heading towards the scene of October's agonies. We were determined to start from the spot where we'd broken our journey.

When we arrived luck seemed to be with us; the lagoon was full of water. Within minutes we were loaded and paddling. We hadn't gone a dozen strokes, however, when the canoe was as tightly aground as it had ever been. Dana's feet were still tender from our last bout with Laguna Madre, and he refused to leave the canoe. It was up to Gabby and me, and the two of us climbed into the water and hitched ourselves to the bow with towing ropes. With its decreased load, the canoe floated nicely, and we were off down the lagoon.

By mid-afternoon, La Pesca was won. I felt like a warrior who had defeated an ancient, dogged enemy.

FEBRUARY 20: *Punta Jerez, Mexico*

Our voyage since La Pesca has not been easy. For the first day or so, we paddled and towed our way down Laguna Madre. When we could go no further, we portaged to the Gulf and were confronted by exactly what we feared most — bank upon bank of deafening two-metre breakers. The noise alone was enough to make me wish we were back in Veracruz. Gabby was terrified. He had all of a single day's paddling experience. And here were waters that would have intimidated the toughest canoeists on earth.

Just after 7:00 a.m., I screamed "Go!" but even before we'd got into the canoe, a wave swept along it, dumping water in through the cockpits. By the time we were 60 metres offshore, the canoe was so full of water that our gunwales were dipping beneath the surface. We bulled our way through three last shore waves and into the rolling seas beyond. Out of the depths of my panic, I yelled, "Bail!"

"With what?" Gabby answered.

"With anything! With your lunch bottle!"

We carry our lunches in wide-necked plastic containers, and in no time Gabby had his open in his hands. "Dump it!" I shouted, meaning that he should dump it on the canoe cover. Instead he tossed it into the sea and began bailing frantically.

In half an hour, he had drained the canoe, and we were riding high. But everything was clearly not well with Gabby. His face had gone from its normal healthy tan colour to a ghastly green. But never once did he stop paddling, although I urged him to take a rest. All day he shivered and rattled and retched, and all day he swung his aluminum Gruman paddle.

FEBRUARY 24: *on Laguna de Tamiahua*
Gabby is gaining strength and is more like a son to me every day.

We entered 160 km of protected waterways three days ago at the big city of Tampico. The paddling since has been splendid. So, too, has the scenery; in the distance to our west are high purple mountains, at the base of which lie palms and tropical shrubs.

Yesterday we spent a gruelling 12 hours on the water. Gabby paddled like a veteran and staggered from the canoe, barely able to stand. He has impressed me immensely and I've told him that if we get to Veracruz, the aluminum paddle he's using will be his.

MARCH 3: *Punta Penon, Mexico*
Here we are, back on the Gulf of Mexico, just 69 km north of Veracruz. Much of our success has been in our improved launching and landing techniques. We haven't swamped once in four days.

The first day on the Gulf, we were battling huge waves by the time we were ready to land. The only way we could even hope to get in was by using a variation of the landing technique that we worked out back at Washington Beach. Some distance out, all three of us jumped into the water. Dana and Gabby took the bow gunwales and I took the stern. It was the first time we'd come off heavy seas without swamping.

Our launchings, too, are improving, though Dana still takes an awful pounding in the bow as the shore breakers wash over him. He puts his head down for the plunge, like a football fullback driving into the line, but the waves straighten him right up and leave him gasping.

The open water, too, has given us some dicey moments. An occasional wave from the east is so threatening that we have to swing the canoe directly out to sea, to keep from being tipped. It's all so strange to me as a paddler. I've never taken a canoe trip on which I couldn't say, "We'll do this today, we'll paddle so many kilometres to such and such a place." The Gulf tells us what *it* will allow us to do. More and more I wonder how Dana and I will fare beyond Veracruz — and if we'll survive at all. I am far from certain that the two of us will be able to handle the loaded canoe.

MARCH 5: *Veracruz, Mexico*

We ploughed into Veracruz harbour late this morning and pulled ashore on the beach right in front of our house, and were soon exulting in a loving welcome from our former landlady and housemates. Gabby's parents had driven hundreds of kilometres to welcome him back, and they beamed with pride and relief.

MARCH 6: *Veracruz, Mexico*
Today we have spent all our time preparing for tomorrow's big launch. Ahead of us are 1860 km of Mexican coast, and we feel if we can beat Mexico, nothing will stop us. Once around the Yucatán, we'll be on the calmer Caribbean and home free. *If we can paddle the Gulf with two people.*

MARCH 7: *north of Alvarado, Mexico*
Up at five o'clock and on the beach, nervous but ready to launch. Gabby rolled up his pants and was into the water to help us. It was almost as if he were going to hop into the canoe and come with us — and didn't we wish he could!

We paddled away, petrified, at 6:30 a.m. For the first time in nearly 6400 km, there was no one between us in the canoe, and it felt very strange.

By 9:30, we were making terrific progress through uncommonly light seas. How long it would last we had no idea, but we intended to make the most of it.

This afternoon we slid ashore on a little sand beach just north of Alvarado. We had paddled 11 non-stop hours, and had come 58 km.

MARCH 11: *Alvarado, Mexico*
Fifty-eight kilometres, the first day out; 13 km total during the next four days. Here we sit, stormbound in Alvarado.

Our arrival four days ago was a nightmare. The seas were rough, and as we reached the jetty at the mouth of the Papoloapan River, the swells were magnified by the action of the shallows, and by the current of the river.

Suddenly, a five metre wave rose to our left. In a fury of spray and confusion, it picked us up and flung us through the air, upside down, into the sea. My first concern was for Dana, but, on surfacing, I saw him beside the canoe about five metres away. "Hang on," I shouted, "and the waves will carry us in!"

How wrong I was. Within seconds, we were being carried out to sea by the powerful current from the river. "Stay cool!" I kept calling, but privately I was beginning to panic.

Further out we went, until we were a couple of kilometres off shore. Just when I'd truly begun to fear the worst, we glimpsed a trawler, not far away. We'd catch sight of it, then lose it again among the swells. As the boat drew closer, we realized it had spotted us, and I uttered a silent hallelujah.

As it growled up to us, one of the fishermen aboard threw a strong line which I attached through our bow loop. The boat took off, but our canoe, with its heavy load of equipment and water, couldn't take the strain. *"Despacio!"* I screamed — "Slower!" But they couldn't hear me. Meanwhile, Dana was barely able to hold on to the stern. With every wave, the tow line went slack and jerked tight again, severely jarring both us and the canoe. *"Alto!"* I began yelling, "Stop!" but on they went. I was determined to save the canoe, and, after repeated cries of *"Alto! Alto!"* they cut their diesels.

They sent down two ropes and we looped them around the canoe, in an attempt to winch it onto the deck. But as the lines tightened, I could see the canoe beginning to buckle, and realized it was far too heavy. Again, I started hollering, and didn't stop until the lines had been slackened.

Eventually we removed the canoe cover and persuaded them to winch up our equipment one piece at a time.

Half an hour later, we were sitting on a wharf in the heart of Alvarado. We'd lost a good deal of loose equipment. But *Orellana* had suffered more than we had. Her gunwales were broken; her aluminum fore bumper had been torn loose; and her hull had been badly scratched.

In the past few days I've repaired *Orellana,* and we've done what we can to clean up our gear. We now wait only for a break from the sea.

MARCH 23: *on the south coast of the Gulf of Mexico*
Many tough days of paddling since Alvarado, and again we are stormbound on a little tidal flat. We have worked our way around the southern bowl of the Gulf and are now heading towards the Yucatán Peninsula. We are two weeks ahead of schedule, and are ecstatic with our progress.

The big problem with travelling east is that during the morning hours, when we do most of our paddling, we get the tropical sun directly in our eyes. I tried sunglasses, but have lost two pairs during the past few days. Even when I can keep them on, the salt spray coats them, so that they need constant cleaning. We're also without hats, having lost ours during a hectic launch the other day. I've been wrapping a T-shirt around my head, and one day Dana wore his rain jacket with the hood up, in spite of the tremendous heat. Unfortunately, we have no way of protecting our lips and noses, which are badly cracked and scabbed. Otherwise our hides are as brown as footballs.

The scenery since Alvarado has been impressive: cliffs and mountains and tropical vegetation. Palms are everywhere, and I take particular satisfaction in the endless supply of coconuts. On the average, between us, we'll consume 25 or 30 cocos a day.

Dana has been going steadily at his guitar and is currently perfecting a piece called "Spanish Ballad." The music flows, and I call out *"Magnifico! Perfecto!"*

The other day, near Punta Buey, Dana met a beautiful black-haired señorita from the University of Mexico. He serenaded her on his guitar until sunset, when she left for home. Later that evening, in the dark, we had a long slow walk down the beach, and talked about our progress and the long journey ahead, and our feelings about each other, and all that we're experiencing. As I sit here writing, I can honestly say that we are a fine tandem, Dana and I. The further we go, the more we want to complete our trip.

MARCH 29: *on the Yucatán Peninsula, Mexico*

By the end of last week, our progress was being severely hampered by coastal currents and winds. As we worked our way into the southeast corner of the Gulf, we also hit a succession of *bocas* or river mouths, which created a fury of breakers and turbulence. The problem arises because the river mouths deposit vast areas of silt, causing shallows which stir up the normal wave action.

A few days ago, as we made the gradual turn north up the Yucatán Peninsula, conditions changed. By the time we reached Ciudad del Carmen, we were paddling calm, shallow waters.

Today, we could see red coral shining up from the sea floor. There are fish everywhere, including good-sized stingrays and giant rays. The other day, we saw a smallish black fin coming towards us along the surface. At first we thought it was a shark. As it slipped by within a metre of the canoe, we realized it was a pilot whale six metres long — and more than a metre across the back. As it disappeared behind us, Dana turned to me with a big grin on his face.

Although we no longer have the sun in our eyes, the heat is increasingly intense, and we've taken to getting on the water before dawn. Predawn and night paddling are a tradition of the Canadian voyageurs. Go when the going is best.

APRIL 2: *at Isla Arena, Mexico*
The day before yesterday we reached Campeche, where we walked from store to store trying to buy glue to mend Dana's guitar bridge. We didn't know the Spanish word for glue, and it took us an hour to get what we wanted.

We left Campeche early yesterday morning and were soon in trouble, as the water got so shallow we had to zigzag merely to avoid getting grounded.

Ten hours of paddling and poling along a shallow shoreline brought us to Isla de Piedras, the Island of Stones, where we came across an impoverished little fishing community of twelve men and a female cook — Mayan Indians. Their shelter was a bleak line of shacks along the back of the beach. In the shallows they had nine small sharks thrashing around on a stringer. We were soon sharing their tortillas, cooked on a bit of flat steel over a shore fire. Later, under the stars, we sat with them around a beach fire, talking and laughing.

APRIL 4: *Sisal, Mexico*
As we round onto the northern part of the Yucatan peninsula, the winds are giving us fits. So much so that for a while yesterday we were not only slowed or stopped but were actually pushed backwards.

These particular winds are called *brisas,* and we take them as a grim omen of what the trade winds are going to do to us when we swing due east beyond Progreso. We could sure use Jeff or Gabby in that big empty second seat.

CHAPTER 7

Out of Mexico

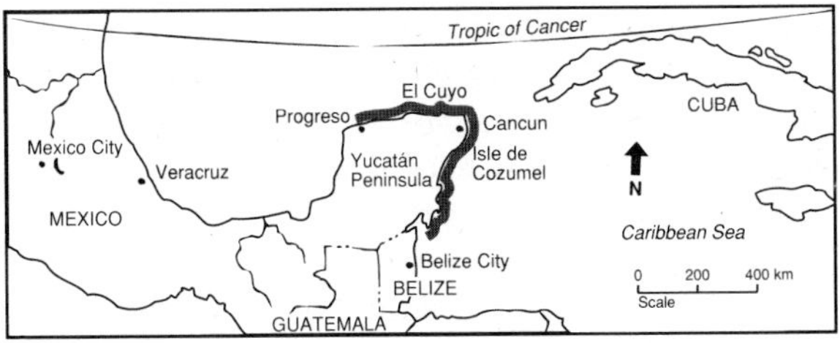

APRIL 7: *at Progreso, Mexico*

We reached Progreso two days ago, and have been unable to move since, because of the punishing winds.

Within minutes of our arrival, a pleasant middle-aged woman, Señora Gladys Marrufo, appeared beside us on the beach, and gave us a heaping salad plate and a couple of icy Pepsis. She was leaving the following day for her home in Mérida, but invited us to make camp in the veranda of a nearby beach house she was occupying. So here we've sat since, in relative comfort. The only thing we can't do is what we really want to do: paddle.

Back on the Mississippi at Memphis, which now seems like ten years ago, I bought Jeff and Dana new Nike running shoes. There is now nothing left of Dana's but worn soles and a few strands of greying tattered canvas. Nonetheless, he wears them proudly, and everywhere he goes people comment on their astonishing condition. Yesterday he left them on the beach, and when he returned half an hour later, they were gone. He finally located them neatly wrapped in a plastic bag in a nearby trash can. Someone had apparently mistaken them for castoffs. Dana quickly laced them on to prevent another mistake.

Last night as we lay on our veranda, a man and a boy appeared out of the darkness. Dana recognized them as the proprietors of the shop where he'd bought tortillas earlier in the day. They'd brought Dana a present, a new pair of white Converse basketball shoes. In the glow of the flashlight, he tried them on, and they fit perfectly.

APRIL 13: *east of Lagartos, Mexico*
We decided to try to paddle at night while the winds were down.

It seems that our last days on the Gulf will be won only if we can gather all our fighting resources and outwit these phenomenal winds. By two o'clock last night, we had paddled 11 km. Then the moon went down, throwing our world into impenetrable darkness. I couldn't even see Dana's outline ahead of me in the canoe.

By four o'clock we'd grown so weary we were dozing off as we paddled. I'd drift off, awakening to Dana's sharp rebukes — "Do you wanta die? Do you wanta kill us both?" It wasn't long before both of us were in a semi-coma, thoroughly disoriented, and thoroughly lost.

At about five in the morning I had begun to hallucinate. I now saw rock cliffs, then a wall of palms. At one point, unable to stand it, I laid my head back on the stern deck, but was soon jolted upright by Dana's frenzied shouting. Back and forth we zigzagged — asleep, awake, asleep again.

After six hours of torment, the first hint of dawn appeared ahead.

By the time we were safely ashore, it was eleven o'clock, and we had been on the sea for 12 hours. We had come 61 km, and our muscles and emotions were in pretty rough shape.

But we were also more determined than ever to get over this last stretch of the Gulf. Another 160 km will put us in Cancún, our gateway to the Caribbean.

APRIL 16: *near El Cuyo, Mexico*

We are back to day paddling, though not really by choice. Yesterday we had covered 27 km, all of which was gained with stupefying effort. One wave stood us right up on our stern, so that Dana was nearly six metres above me before he came crashing down. Time and again, he took powerful breakers in the chest and face.

I'm constantly amazed and dismayed by the amount of unadulterated luck that has affected our survival. Almost every day, we run into some new circumstance that has the potential to finish us. *But we always scrape through.* No one could ever duplicate our trip (I'd certainly never try it again myself); they could have our equipment and planning and willpower, they could have our faith and muscles and endurance, but it's impossible to believe that anybody could ever again have our luck.

With some more luck and some mighty paddling, not to mention slogging through a mangrove marsh and sleeping again in the canoe, Don and Dana finally made it to the city of Cancún, Mexico, five days later.

APRIL 21: *Cancún, Mexico*
The last kilometres into Cancún were a medley of ideal conditions: gentle seas, sugar-white sands, radiant turquoise waters. As we paddled in along the waterfront, past the rows of hotels, we raised the flag for the first time since Texas. How proud we were, with our flag and our bright orange canoe glistening in the sunshine.

During the afternoon, I walked out and looked at the unprotected waters of the Caribbean. My feelings were much like those I'd had on first seeing the Gulf of Mexico: smallness, aloneness, and outright fear. The waters here are deeper than any we've paddled, and will be nearly 900 fathoms by the time we reach Belize.

APRIL 25: *in the Cozumel Channel, Mexico*
Today we should never have been on the water. For eight hours, we survived five-metre peaked

waves, each one threatening to throw us into the sea, and against the high craggy rocks of the shoreline. We eventually gained land at a coral-ringed lagoon, but only by surfing in over 30 metres of reef. Dana estimated that we'd cleared it by about 20 cm.

APRIL 26: *In the Cozumel Channel, Mexico*
We are now 128 km south of Cancún, and our canoe sits on the beach in front of us in tatters — 13 fractures and holes. This morning without warning, a massive wave bounced off the sea floor, and came at us like a train. Dana screamed the alarm. I managed two strokes, and the huge wave hit us broadside, spilling us into the sea. Again we were scrambling to get out of our watery cockpits. Any delay and we'd be on the deadly coral of the reef.

We could see jagged coral protruding from the troughs of the waves. We edged up to the reef hoping to pick up a swell that would wash us safely over it and into the bay beyond.

Instead, we came crashing down on the coral, and our poor *Orellana* buckled and groaned. Dana and I found our footing and struggled to free the canoe, each of us hollering with pain as our bare feet came down on the countless spiky sea urchins that inhabit the reef. But each new wave drove the canoe harder onto its bed of nails. How it crunched and groaned and how I suffered with it!

We'd all but given up when another massive wave lifted the canoe and tossed it into the tranquil waters inside the reef.

As we unloaded, I was hopeful that we'd only been badly scratched. But each time we removed a box, Dana would gasp, "There's a hole! There's another hole!"

I'd never seen such a badly beaten hull. Nearly 11 months on the water, 7700 km, with no real damage; and now 13 holes in 15 minutes on the reef.

I wasn't sure we had enough patching material. I mixed our tiny supply of Mexican resin with hardening catalyst and applied it to the patches of cloth. By suppertime, the resin had begun to stiffen, and we decided to test the work. A puddle appeared in a spot I'd overlooked. With our last shred of material, I patched the 14th hole.

By early evening, Dana was thoroughly demoralized about our prospects. "The way you barrel ahead," he said at one point, "I'm starting to think this trip means more to you than our stinking lives."

I tried to cheer him up. I reminded him that on a journey this long, things were bound to fall apart from time to time.

"I know," he said, "but every day?"

APRIL 29: *Ubero, Mexico*

The morning after our disaster, the sea was calm. Our chief concern was the patches — would they hold? Throughout the morning, I kept peeking beneath the tarp to see if there were any leaks. There weren't.

Our only setback that morning came when Dana realized he'd left his new Converse basketball shoes on a log beneath the Mayan ruins at Tulum, where we'd stopped to visit a great stone temple almost 1500 years old. Ah, well, a little gift for the gods.

We paddled on to Ubero and are camped tonight on a quiet beach, doing our best to relax.

I'm afraid our health isn't the greatest just now. For one thing, we're still suffering from the sea-urchin spines we picked up in our feet on the reef back near Tulum. My hands, too, are suffering. I have an open sore between the first and second fingers of my left hand and can't get it to heal. We're also sick to death of having salt all over our bodies, but we can't afford to use our precious fresh water for bathing. Our clothes and bedding, too, are saturated with salt.

We have now come nearly 8000 km, including 2700 km on the coast of Mexico. The people of Mexico have been more than kind to us. They have sheltered us and fed us and encouraged us. When we doubted we could continue, one of them got into the canoe with us and paddled nearly 650 km. Others came to our rescue when we might have drowned, back at Alvarado. Not one of them has stolen from us or harmed us. They may even have prayed for us.

We feel deeply indebted to all of them.

CHAPTER

8

At Gunpoint in Honduras

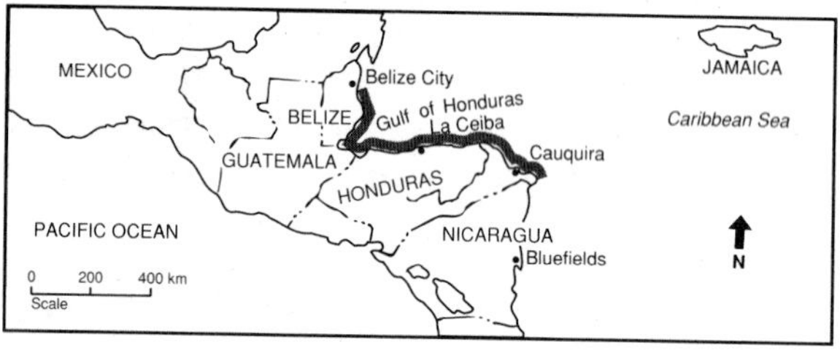

MAY 4: *Belize City, Belize*

We said a bittersweet goodbye to Mexico on May 1st, and stroked into Central America proper.

Our passage along the first 130 km of the Belize coast has been a paradise of favourable seas: calm and clear and teeming with life.

We reached Belize City yesterday morning. We soon found the Customs office, where we met a couple of young men, one of whom works on a cruise ship, the *Yankee Trader.* "Do you want to go to a party tomorrow night?" one of the young men asked. We looked at one another and, with one voice, answered, "Sure!"

Late this afternoon, we cleaned up and headed for our date with the *Yankee Trader.* We had a grand dinner, then a band began to play and we danced and talked and explored the boat. The ship is leaving tomorrow for the Bahamas, and wouldn't Dana and I love to be aboard, free of our own risky little boat for a few days!

MAY 5: *the Colson Cays, Belize*
In all, I got two hours of sleep, but was up at five o'clock for our launch.

By three o'clock in the afternon, we were tired and hungry and decided to make camp on the most southerly island of a little group called the Colson Cays. On the north side of the island was a ramshackle fishing hut on stilts, in which we felt we could shelter for the night. We left the canoe loaded and in the water, tied to three posts that had been driven into the coral.

At about midnight, the radio crackled sharply and went dead. I woke Dana, and we got up and looked out the window. In spite of the darkness, we could see an incredible wall of storm clouds coming towards us from the south. But before we could do anything to prepare ourselves, our shack was tossing around in the gale.

I tried to open the north door but could barely push it open a crack. Peering out through the rain and spray, I could see the canoe had come partially loose, and had swung round so that it was taking the brunt of the waves broadside.

A whole sheet of plywood siding was now

ripped off the shack. Dana shouted, "We're going into the sea!" Sure enough, we heard a watery roar beneath us. The huge waves were now washing right across the island, tearing at the stilts of the shack. For an hour or more, the storm raged, and the floor swayed beneath us. Then the wind died.

At first light, I was out of the shack. I could have wept with joy. Not only was *Orellana* still there but her hull was not touching bottom, which meant she had not suffered any punctures. I checked my lines, and of the twenty or so knots I'd tied the day before only one was still holding, and very loosely.

As we packed up, we kept saying to one another, "It's a miracle. It *really is* a miracle."

MAY 10: *Bahía de Omoa, Honduras*
We said our goodbyes to Belize yesterday and made a daring 22 km crossing of the Gulf of Honduras. We'd had several warnings about Guatemalan coastal dangers — mostly military — and had no intention of stopping in the country. Four hours of nervous steady paddling brought us within sight of Guatemala's shore. Forty more kilometres would take us past Guatemala entirely, and into Honduras.

However, as we paddled within a kilometre or so of the coast, a sleek grey gunboat rose on the horizon. We headed for shore, hoping to evade it in the shallows. But it angled toward us, and we knew that fleeing was a sure admission that we shouldn't be where we were.

As we paddled up to the boat, ten armed

men lined up on deck to look us over. On the foredeck were a mounted cannon and a jumbo-size machine gun. Without a word, the crew threw us two tow lines, and hauled us into deeper water. They cut their engines and demanded our documents, which I handed over.

For an hour or more, we bobbed beside the gunboat. Eventually, one of the crew demanded that we unload the canoe. I pried the tarp off at the stern and began removing the lids from our equipment boxes.

The crew continued to gawk and snicker at us, until I couldn't take it any more and let loose with a tirade in Spanish: "We're Canadians! We're a father and son! We're peaceful people! Every country we've been in treated us with kindness and respect. And now *this* in Guatemala."

It seemed to work, as the captain now stepped forward and handed us down our documents. We paddled off, having lost so much time that we now had to spend the night in Guatemala.

MAY 13: *east of La Ceiba, Honduras*

Our paddling conditions over the past few days have been better than we could ever have imagined — seemingly endless calm. Right now, we're averaging about 50 km a day.

This afternoon we saw a manatee, or sea cow. Dana figured it had been just beneath the surface when we paddled over it, and that we'd surprised it, making it plunge and kick up at the canoe.

The coast along here is alive with hundreds of dugout canoes, or *cayucas* as the Hondurans call them. Occasionally, a couple of young men will paddle alongside us and give us a bit of race, which we invariably win with our steady, heavy stroke.

Our biggest problem right now is the *chiquitas,* the tiny sandflies. As soon as we touch land, they begin their merciless feast on all quarters of our hides. This evening as I worked at my diary, I was obliged to walk into the shallow water and do my writing there to protect my legs.

MAY 18: *near Santa Rosa de Aguan, Honduras*
For the past three or four days we've been fighting huge waves. Hundreds of them have crashed right over the canoe, nearly ripping Dana from his seat. It's so hard to describe our feelings after a bad joust with the sea. Our canoe is so small, and the minute-to-minute concern for our lives leaves us utterly exhausted. We get off the sea, and it's all we can do to fall into one another's arms and hold on tight.

This morning before dawn I realized that I could barely face another day of it. I'm invariably awake before five o'clock, checking my watch, counting down the minutes to the deadly hour. At 5:00 sharp, I yell, "Dana!" and there are a few seconds of silence as he grunts and groans and turns over. I then say, "Time to go!" and we drag ourselves from our sleeping shells. We eat a quick bowl of uncooked oatmeal and water and within half an hour are back in the canoe.

All day, again, the sea gave us fits. Tonight, the entire coastline is a turbulent wall of high white breakers. It reminds me of our time on

Washington Beach. I should probably make some attempt to patch the canoe, as my Mexican repairs have been leaking freely, but I'm just too tired to get at it. We'll continue to bail, as we've been doing regularly for the past couple of days.

MAY 23: *near Laguna Caratasca, Honduras*
Our days at sea remain stupefying, and the jittery Hondurans afford us little peace on shore. Shortly after we landed on a deserted beach today, we were ambushed by ten armed and noisy adults, men and women alike. *"Documentos!"* they shouted, as they waved their weapons. I tried to calm them, and one of them blasted his shotgun above my head. They seemed to think we were leftist invaders from Nicaragua or Cuba.

We argued back and forth for about 15 minutes, until one of them spotted the little blue and white Honduras decal we'd attached to the canoe. "Honduras!" he shouted, and in no time our status had been downgraded from Enemy Monsters to harmless canoeists.

Not everyone is threatened by us, of course. The other night as we lay on the beach trying to sleep, 30 or 40 people came tramping down the sands.

After a while, a woman appeared with fresh-cooked shark meat and cassava bread for us. We sat with these beach dwellers for an hour or more, eating and laughing and chatting, until they gradually drifted away and left us alone on our sandy beds.

The wind has been so strong that at night we've been building a windbreak out of our equipment boxes and canoe. Even so we wake up in the morning covered with sand.

MAY 25: *Ticua and Cauquira, on Laguna de Caratasca, Honduras*
Yesterday afternoon, we were settled on a windy stretch of beach at Ticua. As I whacked away at a pile of coconuts, two men appeared, one riding a little white horse, the other walking. They all but ordered us to move our canoe and equipment from the beach, telling us it wasn't safe by the water. "The canoe stays where it is," I finally told them, and they wandered off, leaving me bent over my coconuts. Dana returned to his guitar under a tall palm. Wisps of Bach reached me on the breeze.

For half an hour I concentrated on my work until, looking up, I saw the same two guys standing over me, one still on horseback, the other now carrying a 12-gauge pump-action shotgun, aimed directly at my head.

Dana was quickly at my side, and the stocky horseman ordered us to carry all our equipment 200 metres to a nearby house. "On whose authority?" I asked. Immediately the shotgun exploded above my head, and the gunman began running around screaming, "I'm gonna shoot your ass! Gonna shoot your ass!" He fell to his knees, waving the gun wildly at us. I could feel my body go cold.

"No ahora! Más tarde!" the horseman screamed at the younger man — "Not now! Later!"

We were ordered to squat in the sand while

the horseman dismounted, approached the canoe and ripped off the tarp. He picked up Dana's guitar and threw it onto the beach, then the guitar case, whose contents went flying. Dana sat unbelieving as his emergency asthma medications and all his other valuables were scattered across the sand.

The horseman began stuffing things into his pockets: my Russell belt knife, my passport, credit cards, compass, watch, money. All our clothes were ripped from their plastic bags and scattered on the sand. Meanwhile, the gunman was so excited he begged his partner to give the word so he could do us in, but the partner cautioned, *"Más tarde, más tarde."*

Then we were marched several hundred metres into a plantation.

As we passed a house where we'd recently bartered for food, Dana darted up the steps and through the door. Just as quickly he was back outside under the shotgun.

The women from the house wailed out their protests: if we were harmed, they'd report our captors to the army. The men yelled back that the women, too, would be murdered if they didn't keep quiet.

We trudged along a rough trail. Dana was wearing a torn T-shirt and jeans and was barefoot; I was dressed only in my shorts and running shoes.

Suddenly the captain shouted *"Alto!"* We were forced against a barbed-wire fence and told to kneel. Our captors went into conference, then the younger one walked toward us, pumped the action on his gun and raised it to his shoulder. I averted my eyes, remorse and terror blazing through my brain. Why, why did I ever drag my son into this? Time dissolved, but the fatal blast didn't come. After what seemed an eternity, we were ordered to our feet. We rose like zombies.

We were told that we were on our way to jail in a nearby town, two or three hours away — certainly a better fate than a shotgun blast to the brain, *if* we had the stamina to make it to the town. We were exhausted from our day's paddle and had not eaten in 16 hours.

The little wooden military station, when we reached it, was lit only by candles, and we were immediately surrounded by eight or nine armed men. We attempted to explain our predicament in Spanish. But *nobody* paddles the ocean in a canoe! Our original captors stood smirking in the background.

An hour later it was over, our fate had been decided, but we knew nothing. I begged for food, and we were marched under guard to a little restaurant. The storekeeper spoke good English, and we poured out our tale to him. He was sympathetic and, having given us bread and sardines, he accompanied us back to the station. He spoke privately with the soldiers.

We were given rubber mats and told to sleep on the floor. Our guardian angel had not deserted us. When we awoke this morning, it was clear that the storekeeper's intervention had gone in our favour.

As the morning passed, our possessions began to trickle back to us, including our passports and some of our money.

Just before noon, the captain and a patrol led us out to the beach where we found *Orellana* half swamped in the shallows. Many of our things were floating, including all Dana's sheet music. His guitar case had been ripped apart.

When we'd done what we could to sort things out, we were led back to the station, assured that the canoe would be guarded. But back in town, a little boy came along carrying Dana's guitar. Dana jumped up and grabbed it, and I demanded to be allowed to return to the canoe, which was obviously being robbed all over again. We were ordered to stay where we were.

An hour or so later, a gaunt American expatriate came shuffling up to us in front of the station and said, "If you think this is bad, wait'll you cross the border. The Sandinistas will take you for Americans — they'll cut your throats."

It is the third or fourth warning we've had about the horrors of Nicaragua, and Dana's despondency is deepening by the hour. A while ago, he said, "We can overcome the sea, Dad, but not bullets. It isn't worth it; it just isn't — well, is it?" he asked, looking up at me.

"I don't know," I told him, which was as close to the truth as I could get.

Last night, just before we went to sleep, Dana reminded me of what I'd said as we were being marched to the army station. "If we get out of this alive," I'd whispered, "the trip is over. I promise. It's definitely over."

Yet, in spite of everything, as I sit here under arrest, I don't want the trip to end. We've come too far. I want to go on, and, deep down, I believe Dana does too.

And the longer I deliberate, the more I'm struck by the fruitlessness of weighing the dangers of the trip against our safety. We simply have no way of gauging what our real dangers will be. We were told that Honduras would be a Garden of Eden! If we skip any country, it should probably be Colombia. We've heard a hundred times about the horrors of the dope trade.

Late in the evening, we were told we were free. Just after dark, we slipped out of town. Dana carried his guitar, and I carried a box of mangoes given to us by some sympathetic townspeople.

We felt our way over the sandhills toward the sea, and soon located our dear *Orellana*. Although the canoe was not guarded, everything appeared to be as we'd left it.

We are less than 65 km from the Nicaraguan border. I think I've convinced Dana that things can't possibly get any worse, and will probably get better. On those grounds, we've agreed to carry on. Our last act before going to bed was to shake hands on our agreement.

Tomorrow morning at five o'clock, we'll be back on the seas.

CHAPTER

9

The Nicaraguan War Zone

MAY 30: *at Puerto Cabezas, Nicaragua*

The day before yesterday, we crossed the border into Nicaragua. We are some 130 km into the country now, and until today, we hadn't even seen a soldier.

This afternoon, as we came up to the pier at Puerto Cabezas, I spotted a lone soldier looking intently in our direction. He was carrying a machine gun which he aimed our way. We headed straight for him, anxious to let him know we had no intention of avoiding him. We figure our best bet is to approach the authorities here openly and ask for safe passage.

"Inmigración!" we yelled.

He directed us around the east end of the pier with his gun. Even before we beached the canoe, 10 soldiers in full uniform had emerged from a nearby barracks, scowls all around.

Within half an hour, we were loaded into a jeep and driven a short distance to a military command post, where a grim-faced officer sat us down and stared at us. His first questions were inconsequential: How many nights have you been in Nicaragua? How far do you travel in a day? Who have you talked to? This dragged on for half an hour, when suddenly he dropped a bomb. He looked me in the eye and said, "What ship did you come on?"

I was not sure I'd interpreted his Spanish correctly. "Ship?" I said.

"Where is your ship now?" he whispered.

"There is no ship!"

Again I did my best to explain that we're Canadian canoeists, nothing more.

"You can't travel this far by canoe."

"We travelled this far."

The interrogation went on.

At length, someone brought in our brass barometer.

"What is it?"

"A barometer."

"What's it for?"

"It helps us tell what weather is coming."

"Where's the rest of it?"

"That's all there is."

"Is it aboard the ship?"

"There is no ship."

Three hours later we were driven back to the canoe, which was a depressing sight. Our little craft had been placed on a pair of logs which had strained the hull, snapping several of the support ribs. For the second time in a week, every bit of our equipment had been ransacked. My camera and all my film were missing.

At eleven o'clock, we were taken back to the barracks and assigned bunks. All over the walls there were revolutionary posters and slogans.

On the wall was a big framed photo of Augusto Sandino himself, dressed up in khakis and a Mountie-style hat.

MAY 31: *Puerto Cabezas, Nicaragua*

First thing this morning we were taken to the office where we'd been questioned yesterday. I complained about our lost articles: camera, film, etc. He reached into his desk and pulled out my camera. He explained that all our film, both developed and undeveloped, would be sent back to Canada eventually. I was furious, knowing full well that nothing would ever be sent home.

When I asked about our documents and maps, he explained that we'd get them when we left.

"When's that?" I said, and he shocked us by saying, "Today."

In spite of our losses, our spirits were buoyed immensely. "When will you be leaving?" the officer now asked.

"First thing in the morning."

"How long will it take you to get out of Nicaragua?"

"Ten days."

The officer looked at me balefully and said, "You must leave by noon today. You are no longer welcome here."

Shortly past noon, we were back at sea.

JUNE 2: *near the Snook River, Nicaragua*
Yesterday marked the anniversary of our leaving Winnipeg, but at the moment we're in no mood to celebrate. For the past two nights, the rain and tides have soaked us, and the bugs have been ferocious.

The whole coast along here is heavily populated by Miskito Indians. We've talked to many of them, and they all express an abiding hatred for the Sandinistas. They can't get food; they can't get work; they can't sell their goods.

Tonight we met several other impoverished Miskitos. One of them gave us a couple of pineapples and refused to take the payment we offered. "You keep it, you'll need it," he smiled. Almost every one of these poor people has shown us the same kind treatment.

And I will say for the Sandinistas that those we've met have treated us with honesty and dignity — which is more than I can say for the soldiers of Honduras.

JUNE 6: *Monkey Point, Nicaragua*
A couple of days ago, we started getting warnings about Bluefields, the major Nicaraguan port and military base on the Caribbean.

As our distance to Bluefields diminished, we considered every imaginable scheme for getting by the place undetected. We could go far offshore and pray for calm seas; we could travel at night and hope not to be picked up by radar or fired at by patrol boats.

About 25 km north of Bluefields, we stopped for the night at the little community of False Bluff, where we met a family named Cuthbert. They offered us a sleeping cabin for the night, thoughtfully providing mosquito nets and a coal-oil lamp so that we could read and write. Many nights had passed since we'd had clean sheets or any real feeling of warmth or security. With the light out, Dana and I lay listening to the rain on the palm roof, and talking quietly of our big plans for the following day.

We had no intention of making an official stop at Bluefields.

By 5:20 a.m., under cover of heavy rain, we were off to meet our fate. Four hours of steady paddling brought us within sight of El Bluff, a huge promontory that drops sheerly into the sea and guards the city of Bluefields a few kilometres to the south. By this time the rain had cleared, and we were clearly visible. We hoped there was no lookout on the bluff.

We paddled in close to the bluff hoping we could sneak by along its base, unseen from above. But as we came in close we saw two tiny figures on the beach. Suddenly they stopped and peered out to sea — we knew they'd seen us.

A minute later we heard the crack of a rifle, erasing any doubt we might have had over whether the figures were soldiers. We froze, then I shouted at Dana, "Let's go!" and we took off like a powerboat. One of the soldiers took off, too, running south along the beach.

For ten minutes we paddled our guts out, expecting more shots at any moment. None came.

We soon had the big bluff to our right and were invisible to the soldiers. I swung the canoe out to sea. The farther out we went, the higher the waves got, and the better our chances became of not being seen.

For an hour or more we paddled in fear. Our chins were nearly on the tarp to make ourselves less visible. About five kilometres out, we swung due south again. If we could get to the island of El Venado, we would be shielded from the mainland. In no time, we were alongside the island, still paddling frantically, half expecting to see a patrol boat at any time.

By the time we pulled ashore at five o'clock, we'd come an astonishing 67 km and were 43 km south of Bluefields. Never had we paddled so hard or long. We'd been on the water nearly 12 hours.

We came ashore at the little community of Monkey Point and for 20 minutes or so we couldn't stop congratulating ourselves. For once, we'd given the military the slip.

JUNE 8: *on the Rio Colorado, Costa Rica*
What a relief it was yesterday as we passed San Juan del Norte and quietly crossed the border into Costa Rica, our eighth country. We have come some 9800 km, more than half the length of our

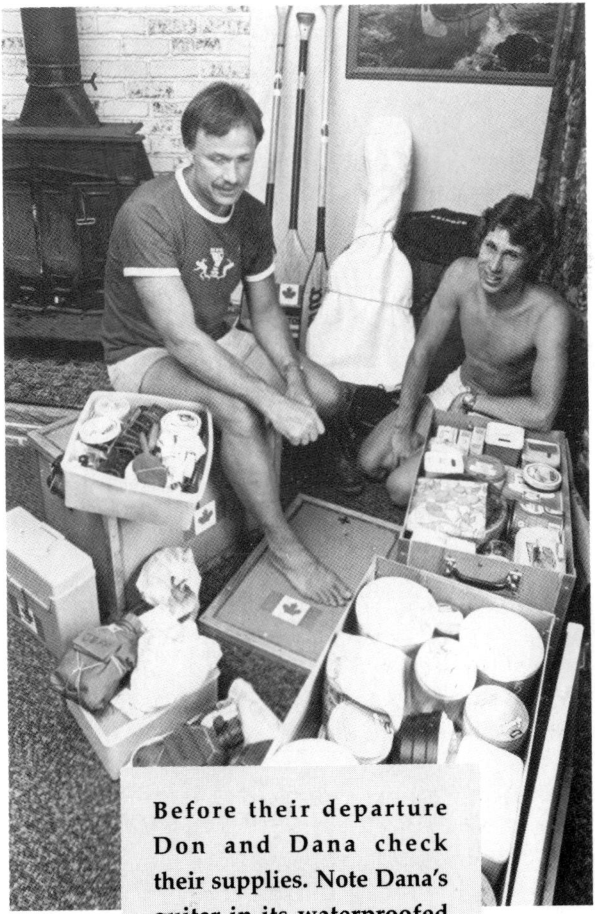

Before their departure Don and Dana check their supplies. Note Dana's guitar in its waterproofed vinyl case. (page 10)

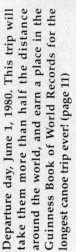

Departure day, June 1, 1980. This trip will take them more than half the distance around the world, and earn a place in the Guinness Book of World Records for the longest canoe trip ever! (page 11)

Don, Dana, and Jeff head from New Orleans to Brownsville, Texas, along the calm water of the Intracoastal Waterway, toward the strong winds and pounding surf of the Gulf of Mexico. (page 30)

In early November, for a variety of reasons, Jeff returned to Canada. A Mexican friend, Gabby (right), joined Don and Dana as a third paddler for part of the trip. (page 43)

Dana practises his guitar beside a grass hut near Progreso, Mexico. Desperate to avoid the wind-driven seas, Don and Dana were soon to try paddling at night, which led to other horrors. (page 58)

Unable to leave a shallow bay on the Golfete de Coro in Venezuela because of high winds, the Starkells' food and water ran out. Don shows the effects of salt burns and heat prostration. (page 99)

With the Canadian flag flying, Don and Dana make a triumphant entry into Port of Spain, Trinidad. (page 110)

Dana poses with some local people. This picture was taken shortly after Don and Dana, using a trailer and their own "horsepower," hauled their canoe 70 km around the Atures Rapids. (page 124)

On the Orinoco River, Don and Dana became extremely ill and had to paddle 80 kilometres to get help. Here they are recovered, ready to resume their journey. (page 129)

trip. It's as if we'd scaled a giant mythic mountain and were now on our way down the other side.

The trip through Costa Rica and Panama was one of the most beautiful segments of their long voyage. Don wrote in his diary of the "dazzling world of the Costa Rican jungle: 30-metre trees trailing endless tangled vines, magnificently-coloured birds and flowers, immense silences broken only by the occasional cries of birds and monkeys." He also wrote of the friendly people living along the coast who saved them from starvation when their food and money ran out.

A major disappointment came in Panama, when they were refused permission to enter the Panama Canal because their canoe was not "seaworthy." Don and Dana had planned to dip their paddles in the Pacific Ocean on the far side of the canal, then carry on along the Panamanian coast into Colombia.

CHAPTER 10

Into Colombia

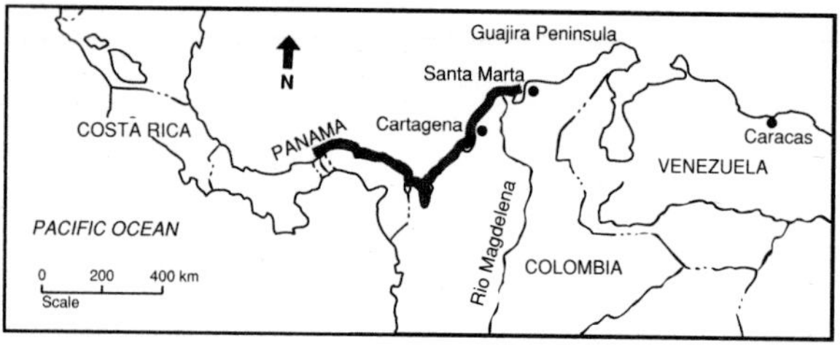

JULY 2: *Punta Goleta, on Golfo de Uraba, Colombia, South America*

We've had warnings about Colombian coastal pirates, who are said to travel in speedboats and to exact ruthless penalties from their victims. We had a brief conversation with a couple of Panama National Guardsmen just before crossing into Colombia. "They'll take everything you have," one of them told us. "If you're lucky they won't kill you." We paddled far more slowly than usual — why hurry toward disaster? But by early afternoon we'd seen nothing but our own paranoid shadows and decided to call it quits at the village of Zapzurro.

It was Canada Day, and we spent the evening in quiet celebration of being the first people to reach South America by canoe from Canada: 10,768 km. By nightfall, however, it had begun to rain, and our night was miserable.

Sometime after midnight Dana woke me up yelling, "The canoe is gone!" The tide had come in higher than we'd expected. I went tearing down the beach to grab the canoe about six metres offshore. Only the slight onshore wave action had prevented it from floating away entirely.

JULY 10: *at Isla Baru, Colombia*

On July 3, we made a desperate 28 km crossing of the Golfo Uraba, saving over a 160 km.

We are now well over 300 km into Colombia and have still experienced nothing in the way of a serious confrontation.

The bugs are after us as usual, and now that I'm without my sleeping shell, I wrap myself at night in mesh bags. I put one on each limb and put my mosquito hat on my head. It's not Eddie Bauer, but the bags keep the bugs out, and that's what matters.

JULY 15: *Cartagena, Colombia*

This is our fifth day in the majestic city of Cartagena. We'd half planned to meet Richie Gage, our reporter friend from Winnipeg, so that he could do a series of stories on our trip. It took us two days to find out that he's not coming. Instead, we've agreed to meet him in Trinidad.

We paddled into Cartagena on the 11th and made camp on a quiet lagoon that fronted several elegant hotels. I made friends with a family from Bogotá who invited us to their hotel suite that evening, for a room-service dinner. We had a fine meal, whose *pièce de resistance* was a little bowl of unidentifiable, crunchy brown nuggets, salty and tasty.

"Do you know what you're eating?" our host asked, as we scoffed up the delicacy.

"No," I said, "What?"

"*Hormigas,*" he smiled — "Ants."

JULY 17: *at Santa Veronica, Colombia*

The Colombian coast is as jagged as a saw blade, and I like to save paddling time by jumping from point to point. The danger is that we're often far from shore. Dana prefers the safe route closer to land.

Yesterday morning Dana grew particularly angry at my risk-taking. A storm was rising ahead. "We're too far out!" he shouted. In no time the storm was on us, and I realized he was right. We headed for shore, but about 60 metres out a rushing two-metre wave caught us. In an instant, we were hanging upside down in the surf, still tied in our cockpits.

When I surfaced, gasping, Dana was with the canoe some 25 metres away. He was fighting to right it, and I was amazed to see him succeed — an all but impossible task alone in deep water. The surf quickly carried us to shore, crashing the canoe on the beach.

We bailed like machines, then lifted the lids

from our equipment boxes, astounded at what we found. Except for about a cupful of water, they were dry. Dana's quick action had saved them.

Soaked and embarrassed, we were greeted by a family who seemed to be caretaking a nearby beach cottage.

We were soon sitting inside, drinking hot coffee and calming our nerves. We paid our hosts $2 to cook us a meal, and as soon as we'd eaten we spread our tarp on the concrete floor of the veranda and sacked out. The canoe sat about 90 metres away where we'd crash-landed. We had taken our valuables to bed with us: money, maps, documents, radio, compass, binoculars, and, as always, my diaries, which have gained increasing importance to me since the loss of our cameras and film.

It rained throughout the night, but I took a number of walks down to our lonely canoe to make sure it was safe.

This morning, however, I found we had been robbed. Much of our clothing was gone and most of our important provisions.

Dana ran off in wild frustration, checking around the nearby houses for any sign that might betray the thieves. I told him he was wasting his time, but he was too enraged to listen.

Finally, we paddled off, heading northeast for Barranquilla, a city of perhaps a million people. We've already decided not to stop — in fact will make as few stops as possible in populated areas along the remaining 650 km of Colombian coast.

JULY 20: *at the Río Magdalena, Colombia*
Things are pretty bad here just east of the *boca* of the Río Magdalena. The wind is howling, the seas are crashing, the sand is whipping us, and the tidal waters are swirling like boiling soup.

I hardly need repeat that we've had some tough times at sea, but getting around the mouth of the Río Magdalena yesterday morning was unquestionably our worst yet.

For five hours we battled the waves and current. By three o'clock we had manoeuvered far enough east to make a desperate run at the shore. When we were 400 metres out, a breaker caught us from behind, sending us into an uncontrolled rocket ride. Twice our bow dipped; the third time, it dug into the surf, wrenching us sideways. In an instant, we were back in the water and the guitar and our paddles and various pieces of our gear had been tossed free.

We spent the five hours between landing and sunset laying out every piece of our sea-soaked equipment.

How terribly discouraging it all was. Twice in three days. If it's not the thieves, it's the seas; or the rain; or the bugs; or the sun; or the police or the army. We're nearly 2300 km from Trinidad, and more and more I wonder if we'll ever make it. It's impossible to stop and rest, as we have to get there before December, when the northeast winds make the coast impossible to travel.

CHAPTER 11

The Evil Coast

JULY 24: *east of Santa Marta, Colombia*

About the only constant these days is the enormous swings in our fortune and our mood. On the 21st, we enjoyed a fine day on the water, and got an excellent night's rest. Great. The next morning, however, we were accosted at sea by a gang of thirteen doped or drunk men in *cayucas*, who made a blundering attempt to pirate us. They were only driven off by a blustering warning that the Colombian government and police were behind our trip. We carried on so brave, so mad, and terribly shaky.

Yesterday in Santa Marta we headed into the steaming city, where we bought new white hats, eating plates, and a pair of blue track shoes for me. Then we hit a snag — none of the ten banks we were able to find would give us money on either my Visa or Mastercharge card. And our next major city, Caracas, is nearly 1600 km away. There was nothing we could do but carry on and hope — and scrounge. We bought $65 worth of groceries and are left with US $40.

Our more immediate fear, of course, is the treachery that we're assured awaits us over the next couple of hundred kilometres of coast. Even the police are reluctant to give us encouragement. "I can tell you anything you want to hear," said a young officer, who sensed we were looking for some sign of hope. "I can tell you it's scenic and safe and friendly, but it won't change the truth — it's a very dangerous area."

And thus, this morning we set out with heavy hearts in the direction of the Guajira Peninsula.

About two hours out of Santa Marta, we heard it coming behind us — the faint whine of an outboard motor. We were soon overtaken by four Colombians, all in their thirties.

"Donda va?" they hollered — "Where are you going?"

"Lejos" — "Far!" we hollered back. As they passed us for the third time, one of them jumped onto the front deck of the boat wielding a 12-gauge shotgun and screaming, *"Playa! Playa!"* — "Beach! Beach!"

Through it all we masked our panic, meeting

their screaming and threats with a good deal of screaming of our own. If we gave so much as a hair, I knew they'd be on us like wolves.

For half an hour, we yelled back and forth, at which point I was fed up. I reached beneath the tarp for my machete, and began waving it threateningly, and screaming.

"Plata! Plata!" they now screamed back — "Money!"

"No *plata!*" I hollered, continuing to wave my machete.

At this point, Dana flipped out. I had never in my life heard him use profanity, but he now unleashed a volley of English curses that turned the air between our boats to a thick blue smog.

Before our eyes, their determination disintegrated. They began looking at one another as if to say, What are we supposed to do now? Suddenly, the gunman jumped down from the deck, shook his head, and they swung their boat back toward Santa Marta.

We watched in shock as they disappeared from sight. An hour later, we swung into a tiny mountainous bay and flaked out on the beach.

JULY 26: *Bahía Confusa, east of Santa Marta, Colombia*

We've made no progress since I last wrote. We attempted a launch yesterday, but were flipped and thrown back on the beach.

We've decided that, in spite of our losses, we're still carrying too much stuff, and Dana has been going wingy, trying to knock off every unnecessary scrap of baggage weight. He's gone so far as to cut away any portions of maps that we won't need.

Nearly everything we started with is gone, taken by thieves or the ocean: binoculars, tape recorder, two cameras, tent, sleeping pad, most of our pots. One thing that pleases me is that, after more than 11 000 km, we still have our original paddles.

Between July 26 and August 1, the Starkells were stormbound in Bahía Confusa, the Bay of Confusion. They soon found that the bay was a centre for a flourishing drug trade. Speedboats came and went to Miami, Florida. At night, a trawler lay offshore, its searchlight raking the beach and the Starkells' camp! In the jungle, Don and Dana discovered a storage shed full of burlap sacks stuffed with over 2000 kilos of marijuana, ready for shipment. Local fishermen warned them to leave the beach, and they waited anxiously for "even the hint of sea change" so that they could launch the canoe.

AUGUST 4: *at Don Diego, Colombia*
When the hint of sea change came on August 1, we were off like buccaneers. We were smacked by heavy swells and fierce headwinds, but as we fought on, conditions improved and in no time we were making good time.

By mid-afternoon, Dana spotted a narrow beach on the hazardous shores near Don Diego. What we didn't see until it was too late was that the beach was strewn with boulders, some the size of ten-pin bowling balls, which tumbled up and down with the action of the waves.

By the time we were safely onto the beach, the canoe had suffered another 15-cm crack, two broken support ribs, and several minor fractures.

We've been camped on this awful beach for four days now, listening to the boulders tumble in the surf. Some of the locals have befriended us, but they all tell us of the dangers that await us down the coast. *"Es muy peligrosa!"* they say again and again — "It's very dangerous!" They tell us that, at all costs, we must avoid Palomino, just eight kilometres away, and Riohacha, the capital of Guajira State, as well as of the Colombian drug industry.

By the end of our second day here, I'd managed to get the canoe repaired, and the following day, with the help of two Colombian fishermen, we attempted a launch. The fishermen pushed us successfully through three waves, but the fourth, a heartbreaker, set us off course, and the fifth tossed us back into the brine. Again the canoe was punctured in several places, and this time the second seat, Jeff's, was torn out by the force of the waves.

Again we patched, and again, today, we tried to launch. And again we were thrown into the sea. We really can't handle another crash — we're almost out of repair material. Fact is, we can't handle much of anything any more — we are discouraged beyond description. Although I hate to say it, I've been wondering tonight if we should simply quit and get out while we can.

AUGUST 12: *Punta Coco, Colombia*
We survived Riohacha, and are slowly struggling

northeast. Several fishermen told us that we'd never make these past 50 or 60 km — not because of pirates this time, but because the east winds and waves would overwhelm us. I must say it hasn't been easy.

The area is so dry, and the shortage of drinking water so acute, that we're down to about 30 litres, which isn't much if we get marooned.

There isn't a palm tree, or any other kind of tree, within sight. Cacti are everywhere, some of them six metres high.

Our only human company in four days has been the Guajira Indians, who greatly impress us with their ability to survive with so little rainfall.

Contrary to warnings, the Guajiras have given us no difficulties. The only time I expected a problem was a few days back, leaving Riohacha, when we saw a spectacular fleet of about 30 Indian *cayucas* under sail coming down the coast toward us. They looked like an Arab pirate flotilla, with about five men to a crew. We got a good curious stare as we blasted by, but no one showed any inclination to interfere with us. I wish all coastal people were as dangerous as these.

AUGUST 14: *at Puerto Estrella, Colombia*

The east winds during the past couple of days have been merciless. They rise with the sun, whipping the sea into turmoil, and don't calm down until dusk. Although we hate night paddling, we realized a few days ago that our only hope for getting out of Colombia was to get as much sleep as we could while the wind was up, and shove off at dusk.

Yesterday, we set off at seven o'clock as the sun and winds dropped. We paddled hard until perhaps one o'clock in the morning, figuring we'd come 30 km or more. A few kilometres ahead lay a small river mouth. We hoped it would be our escape from the sea. As we drew closer, however, we could hear the sickening roar of breakers smashing the shoreline. There was little hope of getting in safely. So we paddled toward Puerto Estrella, 16 km down the coast, guided only by the sound of waves hitting the reefs and rocks.

Within a couple of hours, the rolling waves had risen to four metres, and I had no choice but to swing the canoe straight out to sea.

By this time Dana was issuing panic instructions — Go left! Go right! Straight ahead!

For five hours we fought the waves, until I was sure we'd never see dawn. But finally off to our right I detected the faintest glimmer of light.

All I wanted was solid ground beneath me. As we paddled close to the coast, however, we could see the waves battering the high red cliffs as powerfully as ever. At this stage I didn't care; I wanted off the seas, whether we crashed or not. "Pick your spot!" I shouted to Dana.

"We'll get killed in there!" he shouted back, and before I could say another word, he had virtually ordered me to head further down the coast.

Two hours later, with the waves building, we paddled into a large wind-protected bay, surrounded by cliffs, on top of which sat the houses of Puerto Estrella. In no time, we were besieged by townspeople, several of whom offered us drinks and fruit. None of them believed we'd come from 13 hours at sea. We barely believed it ourselves.

As we sat by the canoe in a stupor, Dana looked at me and said softly, "When we reach Venezuela, I'm going to cry. I'm just going to sit there and cry." For myself, I could have broken into tears on the spot. There's little I can say that adequately conveys my admiration for Dana. Very few older, stronger men could have borne up as well.

I'm particularly proud of the leadership role Dana's assumed. He plans our days in advance, chooses landing and launching sites, sorts out various paddling problems, reads the maps, and issues responsible commands at sea. Without his constant watchful concern for our well-being and safety, we probably would not be alive. I often think that without his guitar he couldn't have held up; on many occasions it's been his only sanctuary from the madness.

Within an hour of arriving, we were fast asleep in the shade of an old wooden barge that was rotting on the beach. When we awakened in the early afternoon, I looked at our maps and realized that last night was a historic occasion: somewhere on the seas in the darkness, we surpassed the record for the longest canoe trip ever. We have now come 12 091 km.

AUGUST 15: *Parajimaru, Colombia*

I can only explain our decision to go back on the sea last night by saying that we were desperate to conquer this last stretch of Colombia, and couldn't do it while the wind was up during the day.

The moon was full, and we slid along through ideal conditions. Our problem was that we'd had only three hours' sleep during the day. Before long, our eyelids and paddles began to droop.

My periods of sleep were ablaze with hallucinations. I'd be barely beyond consciousness when out of nowhere, an enormous sailing schooner would be racing at me from just a few metres away, or the canoe would be about to strike a brick wall, or a stand of palms. I'd be jolted awake, trying desperately to steer away from an obvious collision.

Dana, too, was having queer visions. Time and again, he was awakened in terror by the grinning face of a pirate. At one point, he screamed out in shock.

Fortunately, the seas were kind as we paddled and slept and hallucinated.

In three nights of paddling, we've advanced over 160 km on a total of eight hours' sleep. It is now nearly ten o'clock in the morning, August 15, and, as friendly little Guajira kids wander around our campsite, I can no longer hold my pen to keep writing.

CHAPTER 12

Venezuelan Feast and Famine

AUGUST 16: *30 kilometres into Venezuela*

This morning at about nine o'clock we pushed across the border into Venezuela.

You'd think that crossing the border would be an occasion for jubilance, and I, at least, am ecstatic to be where we are. Dana, however, is irritable beyond belief.

This evening as we lay on the beach, we had a bit of a chat about the bad feelings, and it turned out he'd been annoyed at me all day over my insistence on paddling so close to the various *puntas* — points — with their surf and rocks. I'm only trying to save a few hundred metres here and there, but he seems to think I'm deliberately trying to irritate him. We made up before going to sleep, and I've resolved to be more responsive to his wishes and advice.

As we drifted off, the full moon shone above us, and a light breeze cooled our wounds.

AUGUST 22: *Punta Capana, Venezuela*
We thought we'd had it with guns and arrests, but on our fourth day across the border a motorboat with seven male passengers closed in behind us. One of the men produced a rifle and ordered us to shore. I shouted, "Why?" and right away the roar of his gun shook the air. A shell cleared my head by less than a metre.

Another gun now appeared, and we were quickly on our way to shore. We had obviously been taken for dope smugglers from Colombia, and were ordered into the seatless back compartment of an old Mercedes-Benz that was parked on the beach.

Just before noon, we rattled through the gates of a large military base. For four hours, we were left sitting outside in the high desert sun — no water, no shade, no food. From time to time, soldiers came up and grilled us with hostile questions. We were wasting our time trying to make them understand we'd come from Canada. They seemed to think we were making fun of them. Our documents meant nothing to them.

The worst of it at this stage was that we hadn't eaten in 20 hours. We sat, we paced, we sweated, we sat some more.

In the mid-afternoon, we were told we were free to go — free to walk 16 km back down the beach. I raised a stink, and a soldier flagged down a passing vehicle for us.

By way of contrast, we've met some very fine Venezuelans, too. The other day three little Guajira boys led me back across the sand dunes to their water supply. One of them fell to his knees and uncovered a wooden disc, revealing a secret desert well, from which I was able to fill our big blue water container. I started back, stopping every so often to switch the heavy container from one hand to the other. The boys thought this was a big joke. One of them, who couldn't have weighed much more than 30 kg, hoisted the container to his shoulder, telling me that this was the way to carry water, and the three of them carried it back to the canoe.

That afternoon, I found an old abandoned *cayuca* from which I was able to pry a good-sized lump of caulking tar. I spread it across *Orellana's* weakening patches, and it partially staunched the leaks. I'll make stronger repairs in Caracas.

Dana is at least back at his guitar, after several days away from it during our final stretch in Colombia. He's also celebrating a full year of freedom from his asthma medications. For ten difficult years, he tried to break the dependence, and now he seems to have done it. I remember the days, years ago, when he couldn't walk home from school without having to stop and sit on the curb for a while to catch his breath.

This evening, we saw thousands of brown

pelicans flying above us from the west and landing on the tidal flats down the coast. I've read that they're an endangered species; if it's true, we must have seen a pretty fair portion of the world's population tonight.

For a while, the sight took our minds off the fact that we're running short of food. We still have our $40, which should buy us a couple of weeks' worth of supplies, though not enough to get us to Caracas, where we'll be able to get money.

AUGUST 27: *on the Golfete de Coro, Venezuela*
Since I last wrote, we've worked ourselves into a frightful situation. We have been stormbound for three days now on a shallow bay at the base of the huge Peninsula de Paraguaná.

Our water is down to 20 litres, our food supplies have dropped to starvation level, and our resolve is just about gone. I rooted through our food box, seeking any items we might have overlooked. But I could find only some canned goods, rice, and powdered milk. For breakfast, we had half a bread roll each and a teaspoon of jam, which was all we had left of either item. An hour later, I found a dead fish. The meat seemed firm, so I cut it up and put it in our aluminum pot. If we don't get out of here soon, we may have to take our chances and eat it.

It's almost impossible to convey how isolated and desolate it is here on the Golfete. During the day, the heat, combined with the wind, quickly draws the moisture from our bodies. Our only shade is a little flooded shack across the flats. Dana sloshed over to it yesterday to practise his guitar. I've just been curling up beside the canoe and trying to keep covered. Walking through the brine irritates the salt sores on my legs. In one spot a sore has eaten right through to the ankle bone, a disgusting sight. A little fresh water would probably cure the wounds, but we can't afford to use drinking water.

More and more, our situation reminds me of Laguna Madre and La Pesca. We haven't seen a boat or plane or human being in three days. We still have 50 km to go to reach our portage across the Isthmus of Medanos. If we could get to a telephone somewhere, we do have an ace in the hole. Four days ago we met a young professor, Dr. Douglas Jatem, from the National University at Coro, about 50 km east of here. He told us to telephone him if there was anything he could do to help us on this part of the coast. If we last long enough, we certainly will.

AUGUST 29: *Guasare, on the Istmo de Medanos, Venezuela*

Yesterday morning we were up early, but there was still no possibility of getting on our way. As we ate our ration of rice for breakfast I had a craving for water that nearly drove me crazy. If I hadn't stood up and walked away from the canoe, I might well have grabbed the water container and been extremely irresponsible.

Just before noon I had a curious feeling that the wind had altered. I felt it first on my skin and in my ears. I shouted at Dana who confirmed the sea change. Minutes later we were packed up and on our way.

Three hours of desperate paddling brought us to the little settlement of Cocuy. We were met on shore by a few villagers, who were obviously shocked by our condition. My hunger by now was unbearable, and I dived into our gear for the aluminum pot which still held our fish. A ghastly, nostril-stinging odour exploded into the air. One of the villagers grabbed the pot and threw the fish into the sea. The others took this as a signal, and within minutes we were inside a tidy little house eating corn cakes and fresh fish. I must have downed four litres of ice water. Dana sat for ten minutes shoving food into his mouth with both hands.

I was then taken to a community bath house where two men washed me down with bucket after bucket of fresh cold water.

Next I was brought a white ointment which I slathered over my lower legs, bringing a stop to the itching. Dana has not had a single salt sore — perhaps because he spends his nights in a sleeping shell and has fewer insect bites than I have; the bites let the salt in.

Just before sunset, we were shown to a little sleeping hut made of clay and sticks with a roof of cactus cuttings. We were drained beyond telling. But for a few minutes at least, I wanted to savour the comfort of our little hut, and the warmth and grace of these generous villagers. With my hammock swaying gently, I drifted into a satisfying sleep.

As usually happened, Don and Dana had no sooner got out of one "frightful situation," when they got into another. Now they discovered that they could not portage across the narrow Isthmus of Medanos. There was no solid land for a portage — the salt flats were 15 to 30 cm deep in brine. And on the other side, a wall of three-metre waves crashed against the shore, making launching impossible. They decided to try to reach Dr. Jatem, find a trailer, and tow the canoe 30 km to a safe harbour. But there were no telephones on the Isthmus of Medanos! On September 1, Dana hitchhiked to Coro to find Dr. Jatem. The next day a trailer arrived. They loaded the canoe on the borrowed trailer and began pulling it.

On the way to La Vela, they were met by a TV crew from Venevision, Venezuela's largest TV station (who were on another assignment and just happened to hear about the Starkells). The crew ran alongside, firing questions. The interviewer, Julio Camacho, offered to help Don and Dana, if they ever succeeded in reaching Caracas.

CHAPTER 13

To the Dragon's Mouth

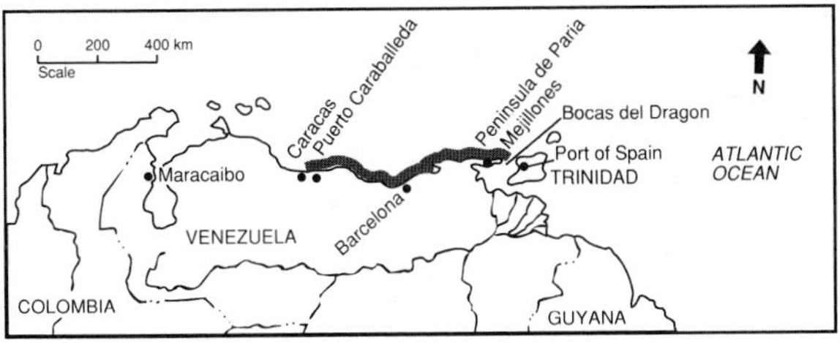

SEPTEMBER 14: *at Caraballeda/Caracas, Venezuela*
The emotional roller coaster is as unpredictable as ever, and over the past few days our spirits have bounced around, building gradually to tonight's stupendous high. We have reached Caracas.

The astounding density of population that fans out along the coast from Caracas began to work on us as we paddled in. The air traffic alone was unsettling — one jet after another coming in over the canoe. We get to a city and have to reverse our entire approach to survival.

A few days ago, on the 10th of September we

reached Puerto Cabello, a fine old Spanish city amid the coastal mountains. When we beached, we were informed by a patrolman that it was the property of the Venezuelan Navy and that we were to move on. But Dana was intrepid (not to mention tired and hungry — we had been on the water nearly 12 hours). "I want to speak to the top official here," he demanded.

Within minutes, we were in the presence of a bright young lieutenant who had us chauffeured to a base camp, where we were fed an excellent beef dinner and given a luxury guest cottage for the night.

Tonight's sleep in Caracas should be even better, as the Port Captain, Vicente Larez, has installed us in bunk beds in his air-conditioned guest room.

The poor man wasn't sure he liked the idea of a couple of dirty gringos calling on him for assistance. But any doubt in his mind was wiped away when our old friend Julio Camacho and his television crew pulled up. Julio had filmed us on our long haul to La Vela and I had phoned him from the Port office this morning. In an instant, television cameras were rolling, and Vicente was the co-star of the show.

One of the most comforting things about being here is being able to have freshwater showers, which will surely ease my salt sores. More importantly, the rest will be good for my eyes, which have failed since we left home. Sometimes, I can barely read or write. It is now past midnight, and I must put my pen down and get some rest. Dana is still going at his guitar.

SEPTEMBER 20: *Caracas, Venezuela*
When we left Caracas on the 17th, we never dreamed we'd be back, but here we are, and in far more luxurious circumstances than on our last visit.

For three days we fought heavy seas and breakers, averaging no more than 20 km a day. By this morning at eleven o'clock it was stiflingly hot, and we were drawn into a pretty bay.

As we approached shore, we were hailed by the crew of a big white sailing yacht, flying the French tricolour. We were welcomed aboard by Martial Beau de Loménie and his wife, Edith. Their two daughters, aged 11 and 15, seemed particularly excited to see us.

Like many others, they had seen us on television and wanted to do what they could for us. We were immediately served a gourmet lunch, after which Edith brought out a medical kit and went to work on my salt sores, which won't heal.

Our hosts surprised us by asking us to drive with them back to Caracas and stay as their guests for a week. Trinidad is very much on our minds, but we're still ahead of our original schedule. We decided to go back — but for three days only.

We paddled 15 km further along the coast to Martial and Edith's yacht club. When they got to the club, we had already been there for an hour, and they could barely believe we'd beaten them. Few people, even intelligent sailors, have any idea what skilled paddlers can accomplish in a canoe.

SEPTEMBER 22: *at Caracas, Venezuela*
Our time in Caracas has been full of everything

we hoped for — rest, affection, good company. The only drains on us have been our recurring nightmares about going back to the sea. We know it's out there waiting, and that before long we'll have to face it. Last night Dana woke up several times, having dreamt he was being swallowed by a tidal wave. He tells me he has similar dreams almost every night.

The next five days, as Don Starkell was to write in his diary, were "far from tough." As they paddled east along the Venezuelan coast they enjoyed calm seas, beautiful scenery, and comfortable beds in luxurious private beach homes and clubs. Only once, in Barcelona, did the Starkells have to confront military personnel with machine guns, who mistook them for anti-goverment guerrillas.

OCTOBER 5: *Carúpano, Venezuela*
Tonight we're camped on a beach at Carúpano, a good-sized port about 200 km from the tip of the Peninsula de Paria from which we'll make our crossing to Trinidad. A number of high-ranking officers have come to visit us. They'd heard our story and apparently doubted its authenticity. I could certainly understand their puzzlement. I try to imagine what I'd think if I met a couple of canoeists on Lake Winnipeg who claimed to have paddled all the way from Venezuela.

Eventually, a truck showed up and transported us and our gear to the local Guardia base, while ten soldiers carried our canoe there by hand. We were given a big concrete room where we'll spend the night.

The soldiers here have issued severe warnings about the *Bocas del Dragón*, the Dragon's Mouths, which is the 15-km gap between the tip of the Peninsula de Paria and the island of Trinidad. The gap funnels tides and currents and is a legendary hazard to navigation. Columbus remarked on its fury in 1498. All we can do is pick a time when the tides and winds are down and then challenge the Dragon as we've challenged all our other tough transits — and hope for the best.

OCTOBER 10: *Mejillones, Venezuela*
The coastline since the base has been as treacherous as any we've paddled. There are no beaches, just kilometre after kilometre of sawtooth points and rock ledges.

One wise old seaman came up to us the other day on shore and examined our canoe with great interest. "We've come 13 600 km in it," I told him. He lifted his eyes to meet mine and said softly, *"Tú es muy loco"* — "You are really crazy."

Just before I sat down to write, Dana showed me a pair of pea-sized salt sores that have developed on his hands. Sometimes when I look at him, I despair — he can get so drawn and run-down looking. His lower lip is one big scab from the sun, and his nose is thick and brown under its layers of baked skin. What we really need is a good long rest in Trinidad, which is now only 50 km away.

CHAPTER 14

Interlude in Trinidad

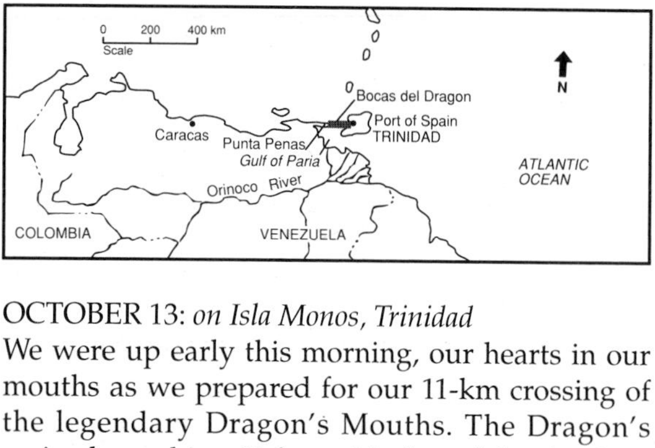

OCTOBER 13: *on Isla Monos, Trinidad*

We were up early this morning, our hearts in our mouths as we prepared for our 11-km crossing of the legendary Dragon's Mouths. The Dragon's main channel is a 11-km-wide funnel for the deep tides of hundreds of square kilometres of the Gulf of Paria.

This incredible flow of water, reduced to an 11-km opening, creates such powerful currents that we'd be committing suicide to travel at any time other than absolute low tide when the waters are at their least violent.

Unfortunately, our ability to judge the rise and fall of tides wasn't as sharp as it might have been. As we rounded the northeast tip of the island we were caught in the grip of an incredible force of water moving north.

Dana yelled, "We have to turn back! We'll never make it!" I knew he was right, and, after a short debate, we turned the canoe 180 degrees and started pulling for our lives against the heavy current. It took us nearly an hour to struggle back to the safety of last night's bay.

At noon, when we were sure the tide was as low as it would go, we made our second attempt. We paddled like demons. After two hours, we made land for the first time in Trinidad. We had slain the Dragon.

We're camped tonight in front of a string of luxury vacation homes in Turtle Bay on the south shore of Isla Monos.

It's still difficult to believe we're here. Just over a year ago, we were high and dry in La Pesca, convinced that our trip was over. What I'd really like to do right now is let out a wail of relief — we've survived, we've been blessed, we owe thanks to so many.

As I browsed through my journals after supper, I calculated that it's taken us 378 travel days to get here, not including our four months in Veracruz. We've come 14 288 km.

As I mentioned, Richie Gage of the Winnipeg Free Press told us he'd do his best to meet us in Port of Spain to do some articles on our adventures. It'd be wonderful to see someone from home.

OCTOBER 14: *Williams Bay, Port of Spain, Trinidad*
This morning, before leaving to make the three-kilometre jump from Isla Monos to mainland Trinidad, I cut a flagpole from some wild brush and hoisted our Canadian flag in the rear of the canoe, for the first time since Cancún, Mexico.

We made the jump easily and, as we followed east along the shore, we could see a number of naval and Coast Guard boats at anchor. On a nearby pier were a number of uniformed naval and military personnel, all waving at us. Among them, I noticed a rather misplaced-looking civilian in a red plaid shirt. He had either binoculars or a camera around his neck.

When we were still some 20 metres from shore, I recognized what I thought was a familiar smile on the face of the man in red — could it be? "Don!" he shouted. "Dana!"

In no time we were on shore, rejoicing not only at our arrival but at the presence of Richie Gage, who'd come all the way from Winnipeg to welcome us. What a thrill it was to see this friend who'd been writing about us since May of the previous year and keeping our family and friends advised of our travels.

He obviously saw things that shocked him: our exhausted bodies, parched skin, scrapes, and scars, especially the thick scab on Dana's lower lip.

Richie had intended to accompany us into Port of Spain in the canoe. We had to pull back the tarp to free the second seat, as Dana had long ago sewn its cockpit shut. But Richie was soon established there, and we began what was supposed to be a triumphal entry into the city.

But we had too much weight up front, and we were soon taking waves over our front gunwales. The canoe began filling up. Richie was soon bailing frantically, and he continued to bail for nearly half an hour as we struggled into the calmer waters of Williams Bay.

Richie took us by cab to the Canadian High Commission, where we met briefly with the friendly high commissioner, Paul LaBerge, and one of his senior officials, Ms. Jean Blanchard.

During the mid-afternoon, we checked into Richie's room at the Kapok Hotel; then Richie took us out for a celebration dinner at the Hilton-Trinidad, where we gorged ourselves on a majestic poolside smorg: steaks, fish, vegetables, salad, fruit. Richie gazed awestruck as we put away plate after plate.

Dana and I sat up late and worked our way through the pile of mail he'd brought us. All the news was good, and it felt wonderful to know that everyone was pulling for us. Dana's mother had sent two white T-shirts with Canadian flags on the fronts. And a Winnipeg outfitter, "The Happy Outdoorsman," had sent two green rain suits which should come in handy during the wet season in the tropical jungles ahead.

OCTOBER 17: *Port of Spain, Trinidad*

Jean Blanchard, from the High Commission, invited us to move into the guest quarters at her home until we got ourselves established. Shortly after we arrived, I took a good look in the mirror — the first in some time — and was startled at how my beard had spread. I cherished the beard for all the protection it had given me from the sun, but it did tend to be wild-looking, so this morning I took scissors and razor and hacked it off. From savage to human being in 15 minutes. Trouble is, my upper face now looks as if it had been painted brown, while the lower part is ghostly white. Dana was jolted to see me when I emerged from the bathroom. I'll start a new beard when we get on the rivers.

OCTOBER 24: *Port of Spain, Trinidad*
We've been enjoying the comforts at Jean's for over a week now and are having trouble deciding exactly when to leave Trinidad. December 1 is a possibility, although the beginning of January would probably be better. We'll be doing 1600 km of upstream paddling on the Orinoco, about 350 km downstream on the Casiquiare Canal, 1360 km down the Rio Negro and nearly 1600 km downstream on the Amazon.

NOVEMBER 2: *Port of Spain, Trinidad*
The high humidity here sucks the life out of me. I'm a little worried about what we're going to meet in the way of heat and humidity in the jungle. We're accustomed to having the sea breezes to keep us cool, though I must say I'd far rather have the heat than the sea to deal with. What a blessing to be done with the sea! If we had to go back to it, I could barely endure our time here. Actually, we'll have a few days of sea paddling as we go down the west coast of Trinidad to the southwest corner where we'll

jump the Columbus Channel to Venezuela, but the west shore is well protected.

NOVEMBER 16: *Port of Spain, Trinidad*
I've been monitoring my health pretty carefully and am concerned about my weight — I'm up around 91 kg, about 16 heavier than when we got here. Dana, too, has put on weight and is nearly bursting the seams of his jeans.

Dana's sores and wounds are pretty well healed, though my own continue to give me problems. I am determined to have my sores healed by the time we go into the jungle, where the heat, humidity, and foreign germs can turn a mere scratch into a major medical problem. Malaria and dysentery are other problems that have stopped many more experienced jungle travellers than ourselves. I have pretty good resistance to disease, but that's probably what they all say — I can see it on my tombstone: "He had pretty good resistance to disease."

Dana has been invited by the local Classical Guitar Society to give a recital at the University of the West Indies here on the 24th. Sometimes he practises from nine in the morning until after midnight. We're excited about the recital but won't anticipate too big a crowd.

NOVEMBER 24: *Port of Spain, Trinidad*
More than a hundred people showed up for the recital and were much impressed by Dana's playing. He gave a fine performance (if I do say so myself), mostly of pieces he'd either learned or improved during the course of the trip. It was an

excellent opportunity for him, and I could see in his eyes that he knew he'd come a long way.

DECEMBER 16: *Dana's 21st birthday, Port of Spain, Trinidad*
The other day, we went to the Brazilian consulate to get permission to enter Brazil. Our departure is now two weeks away, and we're beginning to get excited. We're still a little worried that we're going to hit the Orinoco too soon and find it in flood as we fight our way upstream.

DECEMBER 24: *Port of Spain, Trinidad*
This morning, we visited the local zoo where we hoped to learn something about the animals we'll be encountering in the months to come. What interested me most were the tropical snakes, of which I want to be fully aware when we enter the jungles. We saw a couple of big boas and anacondas, which are impressive in size but won't pose much of a threat to us, as they're easily seen and avoided. The two I was happy to get a look at were the fer-de-lance and the notorious bushmaster. They're relatively large and are highly poisonous, though we're unlikely to see the bushmaster, as it generally lives in dry upland country. The fer-de-lance is brownish in colour, with a lance-shaped head; I made a mental note of its appearance, and hope never to see one again.

We've had a little more of the Christmas spirit here than we had last year in Veracruz.

This evening, we were invited to the home of a fine Trinidadian family, the Keillers, whose son, Phillip, is an exceptional guitar player. Phillip, who has studied under world-class guitarists, showed Dana some techniques which he says will improve his playing. Dana was all eyes and ears and respect. Phillip's wife gave me a big envelope of used stamps, mostly from the West Indies, for my collection back home. We left around midnight, and I stayed up until 1:30 a.m. sorting my philatelic windfall. Then I bade Dana a Merry Christmas and crawled into bed.

DECEMBER 27: *Port of Spain, Trinidad*
Tonight on a television news clip, I saw an old friend, Phil Scott, who paddled for Nova Scotia in the cross-Canada canoe race in 1967. Seeing him got me thinking about how I'd quit my job of 17 years to compete for the Manitoba team. It was one of the best decisions of my life. So often, as the years go by, I think of how happy I am to be a planner and a doer, and not let life pass me by.

DECEMBER 29: *Port of Spain, Trinidad*
The hours are ticking down, and today we did a good food shopping for the canoe, adding milk powder, cheese, margarine, oatmeal, bread, among other items. Dana visited the Venezuelan consulate to pick up our visas for the next two months. He also bought Franol tablets for his asthma — not because he intends to use them, just for emergencies. He's now been off medication for 16 months.

CHAPTER 15

Farewell to the Sea

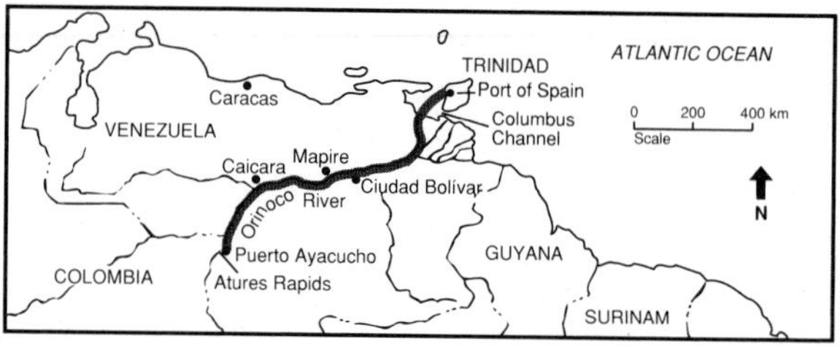

NEW YEAR'S DAY, *1982: Pointe á Pierre, Trinidad*
Yesterday afternoon at two o'clock, Jean's son-in-law drove us to the Motor Yacht Club with our canoe and equipment. Friends came to say farewell during the afternoon and evening but eventually we were alone under the dock lights, as the sounds of New Year's parties floated over us from shore or from boats on the water. Dana took a bed in a covered yacht, and I sacked out on a padded chaise longue.

We were up at five o'clock and on the water within 45 minutes. Conditions were calm as we paddled out onto the gulf and south down the coast. By 2:30 this afternoon we were camped at Pointe à Pierre, having come almost 50 km. We fared pretty well physically for our first day back on the water, though I was pretty well played out by one o'clock.

Dana seems to have lost his resistance to the sun during the long weeks of living in houses in Port of Spain and picked up a pretty fair sunburn on his legs and face.

By January 3, Don and Dana had paddled to the southwest corner of the island of Trinidad. From here, they would cross their last stretch of ocean to the Venezuelan coast and the mouth of the Orinoco River. They reached the river on January 4, and were surprised to find a peaceful inland waterway, with brilliant scarlet ibises perched in the trees alongside the canal, "so many of them that the trees appeared to be in flower." Above the town of Tucupita, Venezuela, they would feel the full force of the Orinoco's current, flowing down to the sea, but for the first few days, their most exciting moment was discovering a dreaded fer-de-lance snake on Dana's guitar case!

JANUARY 11: *on a sand bar in the Orinoco River, Venezuela*

The river here is about five kilometres wide, and its banks remind me of those of our own Red River back home. One thing we're especially pleased about is the appearance of big white sand bars, much like those of the Mississippi. They make terrific campsites, and we're stopped on one tonight.

An hour or so ago I had my first swim in the river, a little wary of piranhas, even though local fishermen have told me we'll have no trouble with them. The real threat is from freshwater stingrays, whose spinal barb can go right through your foot, crippling you for months. A fisherman has told me always to shuffle along the bottom on the way into the water, so as to avoid coming down on the stingray's barb.

Dana and I are in good health. Paddling muscles have tightened up, and our spirits are high.

I've been keeping my eye on the North Star. I read somewhere that it would no longer be visible when we got south of latitude 7°. I intend to test the claim.

We have an attachment to the North Star, as it's one of our last daily ties with home. Childish as it may seem, I get comfort out of seeing it as I lie awake at night, knowing that our people back home can see it and might even be taking a glance at it at that moment.

Yesterday, for the first time, we had a chance to use the green rain jackets that Richie delivered from Winnipeg. They worked well, and we know they'll be a big help further south during the rainy season.

JANUARY 17: *Ciudad Bolivar, Venezuela*

The current is getting stronger as we go upstream. We can't always stay in the calmer waters close to shore these days, as in many areas the shallows are strewn with boulders, some of them six to nine metres high.

We're seeing fewer big ships, less heavy industry, and more wildlife. The other day, Dana sighted our first Orinoco crocodile, a stout little fellow almost two metres long, relaxing in the shallow water alongshore. It eyed us keenly from a short distance away, but didn't budge, probably figuring we were too big to eat.

We're seeing a little more jungle these days, and the other night as we slept on Isla Bongo we were awakened by the bizarre screams of howler monkeys. They were quite far away but were still able to fill the air with the fantastic power of their cries.

A couple of days ago, west of Puerto Ordaz, we were trailed for over an hour by five dolphins, or *toninas*. From time to time, one of them would rocket toward us on the surface, then veer away sharply as it got to the canoe, doing its playful best to give us a good splash. They seem to love our canoe; perhaps it's the orange colour or the bright Canadian flag.

Our camp here in Ciudad Bolívar is on a narrow beach at the base of a towering concrete restraining wall that prevents the city from being flooded during periods of high water. Ciudad Bolívar is the Orinoco's main city, with a population of 120 000.

Tomorrow, as we leave the city, we'll pass under the long Angostura Bridge, the only bridge we'll see in 4800 km of river paddling. It's a marvellously-lit suspension bridge — in red, yellow, and blue, like the Venezuelan flag. We hope to go under it before dawn, for the magic of seeing it twinkling above us.

JANUARY 22: *southwest of Mapire, Venezuela*
We're camped tonight on a sand bar near the north shore of the river. A while ago several of our friendly dolphins gathered around the campsite, poking their noses and eyes above the water to see what we were up to.

Dana is happier than ever and has been pursuing his music with near-religious fervor. He surprised me the other day by telling me that all the paddling, with its heavy demands on hand strength, has improved his touch and dexterity. I'd have thought it would hamper dexterity, as seems to happen with me.

We no longer unload the canoe at night. We simply pull it up sideways a metre or so onto the beach and take what we need from it. This gives us an extra hour or so for the more important things — like enjoying our tea and watching the sun go down.

JANUARY 27: *near Caicara, Venezuela*
We have developed enormous affection for this great river, even though its islands and sand bars and winding channels can give us fits. Our calculated advance for the day was 29 km, though I'm sure we paddled 48 for that 29.

We're tired at the moment and know that the next couple of weeks, when we turn almost due south, are going to be even tougher than the last. We're 360 km from Puerto Ayacucho, and between here and there our maps show hundreds of sand bars and islands, plus four sets of rapids.

FEBRUARY 2: *near Isla Gallo, on the Orinoco River, Venezuela*

Sometimes it seems as if our days have been cranked out of a duplicating machine: paddle, current, paddle, sand bars, camp, dinner, sleep, paddle, paddle. We don't have much contact with humanity. We'll often paddle 30 to 50 km and see only the occasional woman, or pair of women, doing their laundry on the rocks along the river bank.

For the next 250 km, we'll have Venezuela on our east bank, Colombia on our west. We don't have Colombian visas, but have no desire to enter the country anyway.

The books are wrong. We're now south of latitude 6° 34′ N, and can still see the North Star.

FEBRUARY 5: *Puerto Ayacucho, Venezuela*

This morning at about eleven o'clock we paddled into Puerto Ayacucho.

During the past couple of days we've come through four minor sets of rapids, and when we leave here will face what are probably the most ferocious and extensive rapids on the continent — three sets of them in succession, 65 km in all. We may be able to paddle parts of them, but we're mentally preparing for some exhausting portages. At worst, we'll have to portage the entire distance along a back country road.

But first, Dana and Don needed permission to paddle farther up the Orinoco. They received the "stunning news" that their Venezuelan visas had expired and they could not apply for new ones without leaving the country. Their only hope was to cross the river to Colombia, but they had no visas to enter that country either. On top of that, they needed a separate letter from the governor to travel up the Orinoco.

Just when everything seemed hopeless, friendly people came to the Starkells' rescue. Don had in his notebook the name of a man he'd been told about months ago near Caracas — a Señor Paratima. This kind man drove them to see the governor personally. The Port Captain at Ayacucho offered his office as sleeping quarters, and a young man named Christian introduced them to the missionaries at the New Tribes Mission (Misión Nuevas Tribus) *who would be important friends in the days to come.*

FEBRUARY 12: *Puerto Ayacucho, Venezuela*
The day before yesterday, at seven o'clock in the morning, we loaded the canoe and headed out, happy to be moving again. We'd decided to paddle as far upriver as we could and portage when we had to. But by ten o'clock, we'd done more towing and poling than paddling, and by noon we'd been obliged to conduct four brief but strenuous portages.

At the 16-km mark, well into the Atures Rapids, we met our Waterloo — a frantically turbulent stretch of water, which extended upwards for a long way among the huge boulders.

We had a conference and decided that Dana should scout ahead. Off he went, alternately picking his way through the fast-flowing shallows and climbing over the huge boulders like a mountain goat. For three long hours, I waited for him to return; I was sure he'd fallen and been carried off by the whirling current. Then I saw him, slumping toward me from some distance away. I was overjoyed. When he got to me, he was dripping with sweat. His face was pale with fatigue. He'd walked many kilometres and had seen nothing but more rocks and turbulence. We had no choice but to return to Puerto Ayacucho.

We scoured the city for a trailer, without luck. Then it hit me like a bullet — the mission would have a trailer, or would know about one. Within 15 minutes, we had been granted the use of what was by far the best boat trailer we'd seen all day. It was light and well balanced and, above all, available.

We had a wonderful night's sleep, and early this morning I cut a river tree and fashioned a long towing bar, complete with a rope shoulder harness padded with a couple of borrowed pillows.

By ten o'clock we had the trailer loaded, and by noon had begun to psych ourselves up for our long haul tomorrow. We've decided we'll do it over three days. The 72 km will be more than twice as far as our towing trek back at the Golfete de Coro.

CHAPTER 16

Up the Orinoco

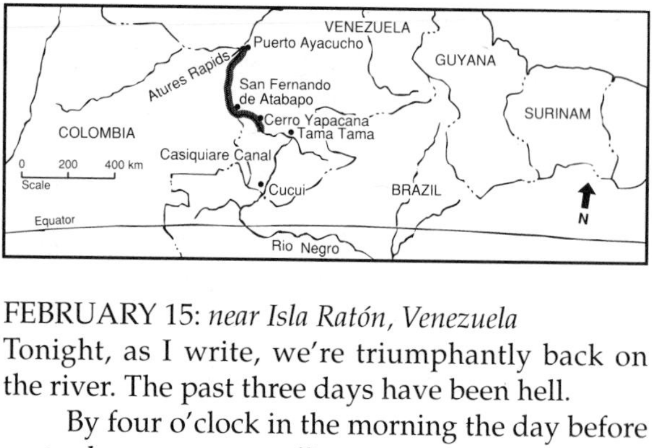

FEBRUARY 15: *near Isla Ratón, Venezuela*
Tonight, as I write, we're triumphantly back on the river. The past three days have been hell.

By four o'clock in the morning the day before yesterday, we were pulling our 550 kg cargo over a gently rolling asphalt road. By daybreak, it was almost as if we were hauling through the mountains. As the sun rose our T-shirts soaked through, then our shorts, and, by 8:30, our shoes. I was sweating so hard that my feet left wet tracks on the baking asphalt.

We trudged on through the dry countryside:

massive rocks, half-dry creek beds, occasional patches of trees.

By one o'clock we'd come about 30 km, and had reached a little food stand by the roadside. The place was owned by a family of Colombians who fed us a fine lunch, and invited us to stay the night. During the afternoon, both Dana and I had long siestas, and later in the afternoon were again well fed by our hosts.

Yesterday morning I was painfully stiff, and hobbled along with a severe limp. Dana was better off. He doesn't have my strength, but his younger body renews itself much faster than mine. Every step was a battle. At times, it was all we could do to gain the next 50 metres, let alone the next 15 km. We'd pick a tree or a rock or a culvert a short distance up the road, and that would be our goal.

Three hours of brute trudging this morning brought us just seven kilometres from our destination. The proximity of our goal perked us up, and it didn't seem long before we were standing on the river bank at Venado, overlooking the sweet Orinoco.

We presented our documents at the local Guardia base and, in return, were given a yellow pass, which we were told we'd have to have stamped at every Guardia base between here and the Brazil border.

By 10:30 we were back on the river, paddling like gleeful kids. Although our legs were rubber, our arms and shoulders were begging for a workout. The Orinoco isn't nearly as wide down here as it was north of the rapids, but its thick tropical shores are far more romantic than the clay and sand we've seen so far.

We paddled 25 km, one of the pleasantest stretches of water we've paddled in weeks, and made camp on a convenient sand bar. We are fending off hordes of insects, which have been with us like a plague since Puerto Ayacucho.

We were told back at Ayacucho that the best defence against bites is to cover ourselves with a mixture of insect repellent and baby oil, which seems not only to poison the bugs but to drown them. Fortunately, the bugs usually disappear after dark, leaving us in relative comfort for sleeping.

FEBRUARY 19: *at San Fernando de Atabapo, Venezuela*

The 16th was a red letter day for us. Exactly a year earlier, Dana and Gabby and I paddled away from La Pesca. Six months before that, on the Red River, Dana took his last medication for asthma.

FEBRUARY 22: *near Cerro Yapacana, on the upper Orinoco, Venezuela*

Every kilometre we paddle takes us further into remote jungle country. We see very few people now, and the animal life is a constant reminder of how far we've come and where we are. Yesterday, for example, we saw our first big group of monkeys. They were a small, light-brown species and did a quick disappearing act as we passed beneath them. A little later, as I was towing the canoe through some shallows, I was startled to see the outline of a stingray just beneath the sand where I was about to plop my foot down. I must remember to shuffle.

Today's thrills were better yet. We made camp during the mid-afternoon on a pleasant sand bar which, within an hour, had been invaded by thousands of bees, which are still with us. We can only hope they aren't the famous South American killer bees. As I write, I have 20 or more bees crawling all over me, including one on my pen. Dana, too, is covered with bees as he sits gently playing his guitar.

Our goal now is Tama Tama where the Orinoco meets the Casiquiare Canal, a fairly even uphill paddle from here. From that point on, our route will be all downcurrent.

It is now dark, and I'm relieved to report that our bees have finally left us in peace, after four hours of siege.

FEBRUARY 24: *on the upper Orinoco, near the Puruname Canal, Venezuela*

Again, the bees have claimed our salty clothes, and I'm standing here on a sand bar, writing my notes in the nude. Today, we were a little smarter and gave them everything we own — clothes, canoe, equipment, whatever they wanted. They've thanked us by not stinging us — it was probably the salt on our belongings that they wanted. For an hour or so, we sat in the river cooling off. This wasn't entirely relaxing, however, as we'd chased a good-sized crocodile from our campsite and were pretty sure he was lurking in the water nearby.

Apart from our bees and the croc, we've had

a safe, exhilarating day. The bird and animal life has been spectacular: tall storks, big red and yellow macaws, and parrots. At several points, the whole river and rain forest shook with the bellowing of the howler monkeys; you'd swear there were lions or gorillas out there.

The jungle here is a massed tangle of large-leafed plants and vines — and towering trees. I'm particularly impressed by the sucker or parasite plants which live high in the trees, trailing water lines into the river.

We have now come 16 000 km.

Note: Our big crocodile stayed around all night, grunting and snorting on the surface of the water. We slept fitfully, with our machetes close at hand.

CHAPTER

17

On to Brazil

FEBRUARY 28: *Misíon Nuevas Tribus, Tama Tama, Venezuela*

Tonight, thank God, we are safe in Tama Tama. I have made only the briefest notes over the past few days. The evening after I last wrote, at Kirare, just past suppertime, my head started aching, I grew dizzy, and my muscles and stomach began to cramp.

Two hours later, Dana, too, began to complain of shivering and cramps.

The next eight or nine hours were an agonizing blur of half-sleep and fear. Our alarm went off as usual at 5:30, but Dana couldn't move. I was too scared to lie there, convinced that, if we didn't get to Tama Tama for help, we'd die. The pain and tremors and weakness were more severe than anything I'd ever experienced. We suspected we'd picked up a case of water or food poisoning.

We were 80 km from Tama Tama — 80 upstream kilometres. I bullied and prodded Dana into getting up, and soon after six o'clock — unable to eat, barely able to stay upright — we launched the canoe and angled into the current. It was the beginning of two days of torture, particularly for Dana, who, by this time, was far worse off than I was.

All day, Dana lifted his paddle as if it were lead, constantly begging me to stop. All I could do was keep at him to do his best, to keep pulling. Several times, he slumped in the bow, and I was afraid he might fall overboard. "We can't quit," I kept hectoring. "We have to keep paddling; we've gotta keep going — just a few more kilometres."

By about two o'clock, we were all but unconscious. A flat rock island came into view in the middle of the river, and we dragged the canoe onto it, stretched out the tarp, and fell asleep. We had come just over 27 km.

The morning brought no noticeable improvement in our condition. If anything, Dana was weaker, and I had lost my appetite altogether. We headed off on a grim re-enactment of the previous day's travels. We were eventually forced into our old last-ditch game, choosing a branch or rock upstream, fighting our way to it, choosing another branch or rock, and so on. By late morning, Dana's complexion was a pale but distinct green.

During the late afternoon we searched for a camping spot, but could find nothing on the high steep river banks. By six o'clock, with darkness coming, we had no choice but to tie up alongshore, and prepare for a night in the canoe.

This morning Dana looked awful — his face was flushed, his head ached, he couldn't bend his back. For the first kilometre or so, he refused to take a stroke, complaining that I'd exhausted him yesterday with 12 hours on the water. And I couldn't refute it; I have worn him out; he is exhausted; he is too sick to paddle. But how else could we have made it to where we are?

He eventually picked up his paddle. For four hours we crawled upcurrent, and about ten o'clock we saw what should have made us throw our arms in the air and shout for joy — or weep for it. On the far shore, amid the trees, the bank gradually fell away into a broad channel that signified the beginning of the Casiquiare Canal. Our battles with the current were over.

The *Misíon Nuevas Tribus* (New Tribes Mission) is located on the Orinoco a couple of kilometres beyond the opening to the canal, and we reached it within an hour. We staggered up the banks and onto the grounds.

As I write this evening, I can already feel the life and health returning to my body. Dana, too, is feeling better and looks better. We're staying in the home of Fran and Laura Cochran, who divide their time between here and the mission office in Puerto Ayacucho.

MARCH 3: *Misíon Nuevas Tribus, on the Orinoco River*
For the past three days, these good people have done everything to bring us back to health. They have cared for us and fed us (at least five different families) and shown us an abundance of good will. And we're more than grateful.

My strength is pretty well back to normal. Dana, too, is better, and yesterday afternoon felt well enough to play a brisk game of soccer with the locals and mission kids. He says he's ready to go tomorrow, and so am I.

MARCH 6: *on the Casiquiare Canal, Venezuela*
The Casiquiare Canal is the only natural waterway in the world connecting two major river systems. It is notorious for bugs, which probably explains why its 350 km length is virtually unpopulated.

We entered the canal on the morning of the 4th. During our first two days of paddling we saw no human beings. Today we came an astonishing 100 km, our longest one-day advance of the trip.

MARCH 7: *on the Casiquiare Canal*
One thing that has surprised us about the Casiquiare is the easy availability of good campsites on the flat rocks and sands. Here we are again tonight, comfortably situated — except for the bugs, of course. For a while after supper, we were forced into the water to avoid them.

We often go for a long time hearing nothing but the sounds of our own paddles. Then something will alert the birds or animals, and for a minute or so the jungle will rattle with life. This morning, for instance, I let out a terrific sneeze, which touched off a long barrage of roars from the howler monkeys.

MARCH 11: *near Cucuí Rock on the Rio Negro*
Yesterday we said goodbye to the Casiquiare Canal and joined the mighty flow of the Rio Negro. The first things that struck us about the river were the blackness of the water (which, given the name, shouldn't have surprised us) and the astonishing whiteness of the beaches.

One of the most pleasing things about our new river is the absence of bugs. The tannin that darkens these jungle rivers keeps insects from breeding. Not so good is that the far bank is again Colombia and will be for the next couple of days until we reach Cucuí. From there on, both banks will be Brazil.

MARCH 12: *on the Rio Negro, south of Cucuí, Brazil*
This morning at about eleven o'clock we passed quietly but excitedly between two white markers, one on either side of the river, and entered the thirteenth and last country of our trip. We were so excited to be entering Brazil that we pulled ashore and took each other's pictures at the boundary marker.

First we'd have to clear Customs and Immigration. What if we couldn't get through?

Immigration officials at Cucuí quickly confirmed our worst fears. We would not be allowed to enter Brazil by canoe. In fact, we wouldn't be able to enter at all without proper papers, which we could only get at the Brazilian consulate in Caracas.

We'd warned ourselves many times that this could happen, but we were nonetheless stunned when it did. To make matters worse, we couldn't even argue our case properly — Brazilians speak Portuguese, not Spanish.

For an hour, we tried to communicate. The officer in charge told us we had two hours to leave Brazil, and I told him we wouldn't leave until we'd contacted our embassy. No way were we going to paddle hundreds of kilometres back upstream without putting up a fight.

In our frustration, Dana and I had been using a good deal of English. Unknown to us, a couple of men who spoke English — a senior officer and a civilian — had been listening in the background. They now stepped forward, and the officer, Edison Pena, asked us politely in English to follow him outside. "I'd like to see your diaries," he said as we left the building.

This intelligent officer now wanted to check our story against my writings. I pulled out the diaries, and he glanced quickly at several entries, comparing them with the dates I'd mentioned inside. In no time, he smiled and said, "Don't worry, everything will be fine." He told us he'd phone the authorities in Manaus for clearance and that we should be free to go within a couple of hours. I shook the man's hand with fierce gratitude. At about four o'clock, our clearance came through, and we were free to go. The only stipulation was that we report to the military and police at Manaus.

We paddled jubilantly away. As far as I know, we've cleared our last major obstacle. Now it's just a matter of 3000 km or so on the Rio Negro and the Amazon.

CHAPTER 18

Down the Rio Negro

MARCH 14: *near Aru, on the Rio Negro, Brazil*
What has surprised us most during our first few days on this wild stretch of the Rio Negro is the number of houses along the banks. Every kilometre or so the jungle will open, and a little thatched dwelling will reveal itself. At first there'll be no sign of life, but as we pass a family will appear along shore, straining their eyes to see us. Occasionally, they'll jump into their rickety dugouts and paddle out to get a better look.

Last night at Madia we camped with a family at one of these clearings. Just before sunset, I walked out through the fruit trees and garden and discovered the family graveyard in the jungle. I counted more than 50 unpainted wooden crosses. The tragedy was that 30 or more of the graves were those of young children — tiny little plots about a metre or so long. It was a sad reminder that fever and catastrophe and poor diet still claim many in these outlying regions.

At about seven o'clock, we joined the family for their daily river bath. We all waded in together and scrubbed away the dirt and heat of the day. I felt better for the cleansing, but couldn't get my mind off those little graves out behind the house.

MARCH 16: *São Gabriel, at the Uaupés Rapids, on the Rio Negro, Brazil*

We've been counting down degrees of latitude for nearly two years now, and yesterday morning, just after sunrise, our count reached zero as we crossed the equator. We put our paddles down so that we could savour the moment. On glassy calm water, we drifted across the equator into the southern hemisphere.

As with most of our other attainments, there was no fanfare or celebration except what we could generate ourselves. So, to mark the occasion, I lifted my face skyward, and screamed out a salute to the heavens. We drifted for a minute, then it was back to the salt mines.

For most of the day, we shot gentle rapids, which sped us on our way to the town of São Gabriel, where the military at Cucuí had ordered us to stop for clearance. We would undoubtedly have stopped anyway, as we were sorely in need of food and maps. While Dana was off looking for the police, I climbed the bank and bought bananas and sugar.

Dana returned after a five-hour absence, with permission from the military to carry on. He hadn't been able to buy maps, but had at least seen some maps at the military base and had been given tissue paper on which to trace our route from here to Barcelos, 500 km away.

MARCH 23: *south of Tomar, on the Rio Negro, Brazil*
An odd little incident last night. As we lay in the darkness, a *tonina* swam up and down the shore of our sand bar. Suddenly it darted in close, and with a bit of a commotion worked a live fish onto the sand within reach of where Dana was lying. "Dad! Do you want a fish?" Dana called.

"Grab it!" I yelled, but as he reached out it slithered back into the water. It was a good half a metre long, and we know it had been intended as a gift by the smart little dolphin.

Today as we paddled, I saw a flash of red in the flooded shrubbery alongshore. It turned out to be a hand-carved native paddle with a spade-shaped blade. I can never see a lost paddle or empty boat without feeling concern for the owner and whether or not he's safe. But neither can I deny my pleasure at getting this wonderful souvenir of the river.

MARCH 25: *south of Barcelos, on the Rio Negro*
Yesterday afternoon, we pulled into Barcelos. We got permission to establish base beside a good-size river freighter.

Dana met an English-speaking lawyer, Anita Katz Nara, who teaches night school. She invited us to speak to her class that evening about our trip.

At eight o'clock, we walked in the dark up to the school. As we approached, we could see that the dimly lit classrooms were packed with adults of all ages and backgrounds. I spoke briefly to Anita's class, and she did her best to translate our adventures into Portuguese. Then Dana played a classical piece on the guitar, which went over every bit as well as my narrative. The class applauded warmly as he finished.

We slept aboard the river freighter, and pulled out early this morning. We hadn't gone far when we began to see changes in the riverscape to lower, swampier shores.

By late afternoon, we were on a stretch of river that offered nothing but swampy shores to a couple of would-be campers. We found sanctuary on an island at a rickety collection of huts, occupied by some desperately poor families. They say they're collecting rubber and are here only temporarily. Dana dug into our supplies for candies for the kids, and when he took the lid off one of our food boxes, a young girl let out a gasp. She couldn't understand why we have so much food. When these people want to eat, they go to the earth or trees or hunting grounds, and here we are carrying all this food in packages.

MARCH 27: *near Moura, on the Rio Negro, Brazil*
The further downriver we go, the more extensive the flooding. In one spot today, a poor little

howler monkey was stranded up a tree, surrounded by water. There he sat about 20 metres up, staring sadly down on us. I only hope he can swim.

We've been making great speed, averaging better than 65 km a day and 8 km/h.

MARCH 30: *Near Airão, on the Rio Negro, Brazil*
Today, like yesterday, we were driven off the water during the late afternoon by the torrential rains of the season. We could hear the deluge coming — first as a distant hiss, then a snare-drum clatter as it moved onto the heavy canopy of foliage where we'd taken shelter. At the first distant sound, the howler monkeys set up an intense whine and roar, which increased as the rain got closer. It was the first we'd known of their anxiety over getting wet, and probably explains the reluctance of the little guy in the tree the other day to jump into the flood.

It rained for an hour, and the thick leaves were an efficient umbrella. But when the rain stopped, the water that had collected in the nooks and crooks of the foliage began falling in cup-sized dollops from 30 metres up. Every so often, a little water-bomb would crash onto our heads or shoulders.

MARCH 31: *Manaus, Brazil*
About 30 km northwest of Manaus, all islands vanish, and the Rio Negro becomes one great open freeway as it bears down on the Amazon. In places, it is up to 11 km wide. Manaus is a city of about a million people, and as we approached it

yesterday morning, boat and jet traffic picked up appreciably. Our first glimpse of the skyline set our hearts pounding, and we figured we were only two hours away. In fact, it took five hours of paddling to bring us in.

We'd never seen a waterfront like it: *cayucas*, launches, bongos, tugboats, great ocean vessels. The whole base of the cliffs alongshore is overrun with shacks and shanties, many of them built right in the river on stilts — or floating! Above all this poverty stretches the modern city, with its banks and business and wealth.

Our plan is to stay three days here, do our chores, and try to get some rest for our big haul down the Amazon.

Everywhere we've been today, we've been stared at. Again, we've been reminded of how bleached and sun-scorched and weathered we are. The equatorial sun has been so strong, it's burnt right through our tans.

We've managed to get through to Richie Gage at the Free Press back home. He says that the Free Press is likely to send him to Belém to meet us at the beginning of May. He also says they'll probably pay to fly our canoe home, in appreciation of our stories. I told him we'd be in Belém on May 1st, no ifs or buts.

CHAPTER 19

On the Amazon

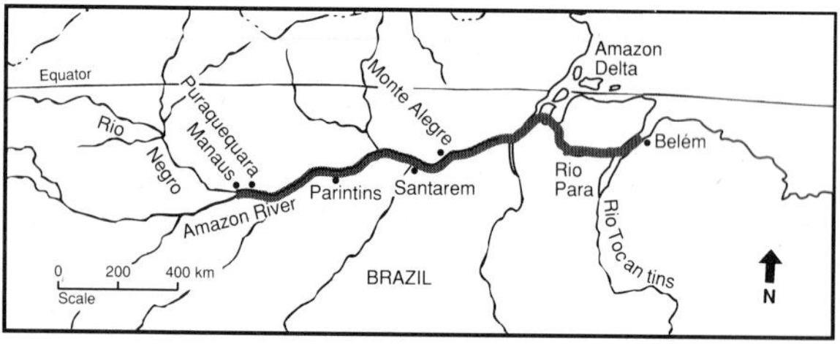

APRIL 4: *at the Nuevas Tribus Mission, Puraquequara, Brazil*

The meeting of the Rio Negro and Amazon is a great marbled swirl of black and brown water, black from the Negro, brownish-yellow from the Amazon. Yesterday we crossed that swirl and entered the mythic river that will take us to the end of our journey.

The facts about the Amazon are staggering: it is 6437 km long and one day's discharge into the seas is said to be the equivalent of a nine-year supply of fresh water for New York City. The river supports over 2000 species of fish and the plants and trees along its banks supply half the world's oxygen. It is the largest river on the planet.

The current moved us briskly, and in three hours we'd reached one of the schools of the *Misíon Nuevas Tribus*. The Americans and Canadians who teach here seemed glad to see us. The rest will be beneficial after our hectic days in Manaus. All along, we've made the mistake of thinking we'd be able to rest in the cities.

The highlight of my afternoon was a visit from one of the schoolboys who brought me a live 15-cm piranha he'd just caught. "Are these guys dangerous?" I asked him.

"Naw," he said, "they swim in the deep water; they don't bother anyone."

He pulled the fish's lips back to show me its frightful triangular teeth. "Watch this," he said, and he pulled a thick piece of wicker out of the back of an old chair. He placed it crossways between the piranha's jaws. and, snap, it was clipped as neatly as if it had been cut with a knife.

APRIL 9: *São Agostinho, on the north shore of the Amazon, Brazil*

One thing that has impressed us about the Amazon is the density of population along its banks; every day we see dozens of homes and ranches. Compared to the Rio Negro or the Orinoco, there's relatively little jungle or animal life. Certainly little romance. I imagine things are different on the isolated upper river, but on these stretches we see far more trade boats than *toninas*, far more cattle than crocodiles.

Because of the flooding, our strategy has been to get on the water early and get off early, so that we have plenty of time to find dry shelter.

APRIL 10: *Parintins, on the Amazon, Brazil*
It has been raining off and on for weeks now. In places we see creeks and small rivers that would normally be flowing into the Amazon but are actually flowing backwards because of the great volume of river water. The floodwaters tear up chunks of shore vegetation and send them out onto the river as floating islands. The other day we pulled the canoe onto one where the grass was almost a metre high — we ate our supper as we drifted along.

The closer we get to the big population centres and "civilization," the less we're trusted. Yesterday, in our search for a place to sleep, we were turned down at three different dwellings. Today, it was four. Yesterday, we finally set ourselves up in an open shelter by a Catholic church. But we'd no sooner erected our bug house than three men and three boys appeared out of the jungle. It took us 45 minutes to convince them that we hadn't come to burn down their church.

APRIL 14: *near Monte Alegre, on the Amazon River, Brazil*
The river is at least eight kilometres wide here, and we're seeing an increasing number of floating islands. The curious thing about the islands is that they're often moving at a better clip than we are. We figure they have hanging roots that pick up the sub-surface currents, while our high-riding

canoe allows much of the strength of the current to slip beneath us. Paddling into headwinds, we'll often pull in behind one of these islands, getting both the advantage of its slipstream and a bit of protection from the wind.

APRIL 17: *Ilha Oroboca, on the Amazon River, Brazil*
After two years of not knowing whether we were ever going to get to our destination, we're finally beginning to relax and let up a little. Dana seems to be taking our success in stride, but I'm afraid I'm a little more vulnerable to it.

It's ironic that the power of the Amazon is almost forcing the kilometres on us. We get out there in the big current, and away we go. We don't want to get to Belém before May 1st, which means that, with 500 km remaining, we have only to travel a little more than 30 km a day. Today, however, we came 60 km and still quit early.

APRIL 20: *in the canals of the Amazon Delta, Brazil*
Unlike the mouth of the St. Lawrence River in Canada, the Amazon's mouth is congested by a massive delta, intricately traversed by hundreds of narrow canals. Today we paddled into the southern reaches of the delta on the narrow Tajapuro Canal, which is about 400 metres wide and richly bordered by jungle.

The tides in this area rise as high as three metres, forcing the inhabitants of the delta to live most of their outdoor hours on water. Everyone paddles — grandmothers, grandfathers, and youngsters no older than five or six. Most of them are shy and pretend lack of interest in us, though we can tell by their expressions that they've never seen gringos quite like us, or a canoe like *Orellana*. When we pass a house, as many as eight or ten people will crowd a window or door to stare at us.

Our shelter tonight is a beaten-down old shack, whose only selling point is the stand of coconut palms behind it. The place is crawling with 20-cm green and brown lizards. They evidently have no fear of man, as one of them just leapt onto Dana and is walking all over him, placidly poking and sniffing. We're only 80 km from the port of Breves, our last planned stop before the final push to Belém. My feet have not felt shoes in over three weeks.

APRIL 25: *near Ilha Coroca, on the Amazon Delta, Brazil*

I suppose Richie Gage will be leaving Winnipeg in a day or so for our rendezvous on the 1st of May. He'll want to be in Belém a few days in advance, so he can get settled and possibly come out to meet us on the Rio do Pará.

All day, we've paddled the north shore of the Pará, and are holed up tonight at an isolated river school. Like all other buildings around here, the 50-desk school is built on stilts — at the moment the tide is just beneath its floorboards. It has several outbuildings, including a woodworking shop and a little home for the teacher. Naturally, the kids come by boat, but, as today is Sunday, there's nobody around.

About an hour after we went to bed in the woodworking shop, we heard a slow-chugging river launch approaching the docks. Before we were properly awake, five Brazilian soldiers clomped into our quarters, holding spotlights on us. "Are you hippies?" one of them demanded in Portuguese.

"No hippies!" I said.

Our documents had a stunning effect on them — they were suddenly very respectful and apologetic. Was there anything they could do for us? Never one to turn down an opportunity, I requested that they contact the British consulate in Belém and inform them of our impending arrival. Of course, no problem, yes, yes.

APRIL 27: *near Ilha do Capim, on the Amazon Delta, Brazil*

The trip has brought Dana and me close in so many ways but even now at the end we haven't fully resolved our differences. This morning before dawn as we prepared to paddle, I issued one instruction too many, and Dana got upset. For an hour or more, he paddled in his own little world, and I in mine.

About two o'clock, we pulled up at a big shaky river house, where a warm-hearted man named Jibuzcio came striding down an elevated walkway to meet us. His wife and six children soon joined him. They invited us to stay.

When Dana and I had bathed and shampooed, I asked Jibuzcio if he had a razor. *"Sim,"* he said, and produced a rusty old razor blade fastened with thread to a popsicle stick. There was no way I could shave with the thing.

"Will you shave me?" I said to Jibuzcio.

"Sim," he said, and in no time I was seated in the main room of the house with my head back. For fifteen minutes, Jibuzcio scratched away at my beard, throwing the scratchings out the window into the river.

Our location here is so beautiful with its jungle and calm waters that I hated to see the darkness coming on. Nonetheless, by seven o'clock we were nestled inside with the lamps glowing.

As I lie here in my comfortable hammock, I'm thinking about how well we've adapted to our nomadic way of life; it's going to be very difficult to go back to civilization. Of course, it's much easier to write such things now than it would have been on the coasts of Honduras or Colombia. I do know that when we get home I'm going to need several weeks of isolation before returning to the more predictable way of life.

In the meantime, I'm enjoying a tremendous sense of personal achievement. I'm unashamedly proud to have come all this way by canoe. We have come in the back door and have lived with the real people of the rivers, lagoons, and coasts. At the moment, I'm wondering whether Richie Gage will be there to meet us in Belém. It'll be a help to us if he is. If not, of course, we'll do what we've learned to do best — depend on ourselves.

For the time being all we can do is stay cool and try to keep the lid on. So far, Dana's doing a much better job of it than I am. I'm surprised, in fact, at how little emotion he's shown about the ending of the trip. Maybe he's not sure what emotion to show. Maybe I'm not either.

APRIL 30: *at Ilha Jararaca, northwest of Belém, Brazil*

We paddled most of the morning in a thick rainy fog, which, at times, limited our view to about a hundred metres. But just after eleven o'clock, the fog lifted briefly. "There it is, Dad," said Dana quietly. Across the Baía de Guajara, maybe a dozen kilometres away, was the ghost-like skyline of our golden city — we had reached Belém. What a thrill to see this city, which, over the past dozen years, has become a magical place for us. Curiously enough, I didn't have much to say about my feelings. What I really wanted to know were Dana's feelings; but he, too, was pretty guarded.

Right now it's dark, and I'm looking across the water to the city lights, which sparkle like a long string of jewels. We've seen nothing like it since Port of Spain. The water catches the lights, and I feel as if I could reach out and touch them. I'm tired at the moment, but can't seem to bring myself to go to bed. After so many months, it's all come down to a matter of hours. I want to savour them.

CHAPTER 20

Journey's End

MAY 1: *Belém, Brazil*
We were up briskly at dawn, but spent the next three hours in slow motion, getting ready for our triumphal entry into Belém. It was as if we didn't want to go. We bathed and shampooed and dressed up smartly in our Canadian-flag T-shirts.

Dozens of ocean freighters were docked along the big piers of the harbour, and as we paddled toward them we kept a sharp eye out for Richie, who surely had to be somewhere on the waterfront. We cruised slowly along beside the boats, asking anybody we could see if they'd spotted a Canadian on the docks during the past day or so. Nobody had, and by two o'clock the truth had begun to dawn on us. We were on our own. We'd come 19 507 km, and there wasn't a soul here to greet us. We continued along the waterfront, and then, for a few minutes, we just sat in the canoe, in a kind of unbelieving numbness. Our trip was over.

We still had to get home, however. Beginning to think practically again, I said to Dana, "Let's paddle over to that Dutch freighter and see if anybody speaks English." The ship, the *Saba*, was from Rotterdam. A strapping blond Dutchman emerged from the ship onto the concrete pier. We called to him in English, and, sure enough, he answered us in our own language. His name was Willem; he was the *Saba's* second officer. In no time, we were aboard the freighter enjoying a soft drink.

The *Saba's* shipping agent happened to be the acting British consul in Belém, the very man we needed to find. "Yes," he said matter-of-factly, "I have a letter for you in my office and a message from a reporter in Winnipeg, advising you that he can't get here to meet you."

I guess deep down we'd still hoped to locate Richie, and the news hit us hard. We'd counted so much on the *Free Press* helping us get the canoe back to Canada, as Richie said they might. What would we do with it now? The immediate problem was to find storage for it while we figured out our next move. How were we going to get home?

Willem went off to talk to the ship's captain, returning with surprising news. The *Saba* would be sailing for Puerto Rico in nine or ten days, after a trip up the Amazon, and Captain Schaap would be happy to take us to Puerto Rico if he could get permission from the shipping agent, St. Roas.

While this was unfolding, poor *Orellana* was tied to the *Saba's* side, taking a pounding against the freighter's metal hull. We expressed our concern, and, within seconds, Willem was in the water with a cargo net, gasping and sputtering as he fitted the thing carefully around *Orellana's* hull. In a matter of minutes, the canoe rose from the sea like a big orange goldfish and was plunked down on deck. *Orellana* had landed.

We ate our supper with the crew and officers and, in the early evening, Willem informed us that the shipping agent, St. Roas, had declined us permission to travel up the Amazon aboard the *Saba*. There are insurance regulations that apparently can't be breached. Seagoing vessels are less restricted, however, and Captain Schaap has since told us that if we aren't out of Belém by the time he returns, we can sail on the *Saba* to Puerto Rico on the eighth or ninth.

This is wonderfully reassuring for us. We've been in port fewer than eight hours, and our travel problems are well on their way to being solved. All we have to do is find a place to stay until the eighth.

I am lying here tonight in my berth thinking back over two incredible years of travel. In many ways it all seems like a dream, from which I'm quickly waking up. Our arrival here this morning was a pretty stark reveille, and I won't deny that it would have been nice to have somebody here to meet us. Then again, we've been on our own since Veracruz, Mexico — why should it be any different at the end? We deserve our fate; we've come too far.

MAY 4: *Belém, Brazil*
The day after our arrival, St. Roas moved our canoe and equipment to a fenced-in storage area on the docks and drove us into the city, where we found a room in the Hotel Milano. From our window we can see out over the thousands of red-tiled roofs of Belém. In the distance are the docks and harbour. Everything seems unreal. We sit in our room here or go out and walk the streets, trying to make ourselves at home. But, for the most part, we feel lost.

We visited the shipping agent's office this afternoon. While we were waiting to speak to St. Roas, we were handed an official-looking letter from the Canadian embassy in Brasília congratulating us on our safe arrival and the successful completion of "this most important voyage."

MAY 5: *Belém, Brazil*
This morning, we moved to another hotel, a little less expensive than the Milano. For most of the day we walked the streets and, in the late evening, went to an outdoor restaurant/bar where we sat for a couple of hours drinking soft drinks. The wild night life of Belém swirled around us.

When we got home we discovered that our passports were missing. We won't be able to board the *Saba* without passports.

MAY 6: *Belém, Brazil*
After a frustrating morning trying to get through to the Canadian consulate in Brasília, I reached a

Mr. Freed, who said he'd phone Ottawa immediately to get clearance to issue us emergency documents. We're to phone him back at eight o'clock tomorrow morning.

MAY 7: *Belém, Brazil*
Our emergency passports have been issued, and are supposed to reach us by mail within a day or two.

We ate at the Malouka Restaurant tonight, and heard some good Brazilian music. Dana sat in with the band for a while, then gave a half-hour solo performance — he got good applause.

MAY 8: *Belém, Brazil*
Today, as I was looking around the Belém tourist bureau, I felt a gentle tap on my shoulder — I could have the passports back for 3600 cruzeiros, about US$20.

As our new passports hadn't arrived from Brasília, I wasn't about to turn my back on the deal. But I told them that we had new passports and that the old ones were useless to us except as souvenirs.

We haggled for a few minutes, and I gave them 200 cruzeiros, about $1.10, and walked away with our passports. I relayed the news at once to the Canadian Embassy in Brasília.

MAY 10: *Belém, Brazil*
The *Saba* came in yesterday with a cargo of Brazilian hardwood, and we boarded in the late afternoon with our equipment and canoe. We were to be part of the working crew and would

spend our days on board chipping paint from the steel decks and fixtures, and repainting them. It's apparently a constant requirement aboard these old freighters and isn't a popular job among regular crew members.

At about eleven o'clock tonight, the port pilot came aboard, and the big diesel engines sounded below. I stood at the rail as we slid out of the harbour towards the dark Atlantic. We're going home.

MAY 17: *aboard the* Saba

This morning, after two days of waiting offshore, we entered the harbour at La Guanta, Venezuela. The *Saba's* orders have changed to our advantage: after our stop in Puerto Rico, we sail to Haiti, then on to Gulfport, Mississippi, from which Dana and I can easily make our own way to Winnipeg.

These long days at sea are not easy. The paint chipping is hard work, and the evenings tend to be long and lonely. For the most part, when the work day is over, I go up into the bow and watch the sea go by — sometimes for hours.

MAY 26: *aboard the* Saba

It is now 16 days since we boarded the *Saba*, and I've gained half a kilogram for each day aboard. At this rate, I'll weigh over 90 kg by the time we get home. The ship's meals are terrific.

We made a brief stop on the 20th in San Juan, Puerto Rico, and another in Port-au-Prince, Haiti, on the 23rd. At the moment, we're about 120 km off the north coast of Cuba.

Tonight on television, we watched a Cuban

baseball game from Havana. Afterwards, I went to my favourite spot on the bow deck and stared out into the darkness. I can barely look at the sea, barely listen to it, without being reminded of our noble, feeble effort by canoe.

MAY 30: *aboard the* Saba
It's 6:30 p.m., and we're anchored off the Mississippi coast. Through the binoculars, I can see dozens of sailboats and windsurfers on the waters off Gulfport. The *Saba's* expected cargo, a load of dynamite, hasn't reached port yet, and we won't be given permission to dock until it does.

Just now, a tired swallow set down on deck and made friends with Dana, who I sometimes think is the reincarnation of St. Francis. Dana tried to feed the little thing, but all it wanted was to sit for a while on his shoulder, then his head. Eventually, it took off, its strength renewed.

JUNE 1: *aboard the* Saba
Two years ago today, we left Winnipeg. We are still waiting for orders to enter port.

JUNE 2: *Gulfport, Mississippi*
Finally landed after three days of waiting. Said our goodbyes to the ship's crew and immediately searched out a Mississippi Motor License bureau, where I managed to get a driver's licence, since my Manitoba licence is no longer valid.

Late this afternoon, we rented a good-sized station wagon and loaded *Orellana* on top. By early evening, we were on the road.

JULY 5: *Grand Forks, North Dakota*
What's left to say? We pulled into Grand Forks this morning and dropped off our U-drive. We had contacted Jeff by phone, and, just as we left the car-rental agency, I spotted him coming down the road in my old red Datsun.

I have no idea how he felt as he got out of the car and came towards us. I have no idea how Dana felt. There were tears that needed crying, but, at that moment, none of us had a mind to cry them. We said hello, and I took Jeff in a powerful embrace, and then he embraced Dana. And that was about it. We loaded the car and headed north.

Epilogue

Since returning from South America, Don has given numerous slide lectures on his and Dana's travels. He said recently, "Our trip taught us an awful lot about how small we are in the broad scope of things — and about the importance of faith and determination in overcoming that smallness.... From facing death so many times, we gained a whole new understanding of the fragility and value of life."

Don now organizes cycling tours for people over fifty. He still lives in Winnipeg and still enjoys canoeing. In 1986 he canoed from Vancouver to Ketchikan, Alaska.

Within weeks of returning to Winnipeg, Dana Starkell won top prize in the Senior Classical Guitar category of the Manitoba Music Festival. He has since released three classical-guitar records, and is at work on a fourth. He gives regular concerts, and plays frequently in Winnipeg restaurants and clubs and also participates in the Manitoba Arts Council's Artists in the Schools program. He owns a house in the north end of Winnipeg, and has no plans for another canoe adventure, although he, too, enjoys cycling. Dana says that his strongest motivation for the trip was his health. "This spring was my ninth anniversary of being free of medication," he told us.

Several months after his return from Veracruz, Mexico, Jeff Starkell began two years of electronics-technology studies at Red River Community College, Winnipeg. On graduation, he worked for two years as a technician for Manitoba Hydro, resigning in 1985 to enrol in Lakehead University's electrical-engineering program. He now lives near Toronto, where he works for Ontario Hydro.

Gabby Delgado is a marine engineer in Veracruz, Mexico. During the summer of 1989 he, his wife, and three-year-old son drove to Manitoba to visit Don and Dana Starkell. Their car broke down in Texas and they push-started it all the way to Winnipeg.